D0894140

*Coleridge
and the
Power of Love*

Coleridge
and the
Power of Love

J. ROBERT BARTH, S.J.

University of Missouri Press
Columbia, 1988

University of Missouri Press, Columbia, Missouri 65211
Printed and bound in the United States of America

Library of Congress Cataloging-in-Publication Data

Barth, J. Robert.
    Coleridge and the power of love / J. Robert Barth.
        p. cm.

    Bibliography: p.
    Includes index.
    ISBN 0-8262-0694-8 (alk. paper)
    1. Coleridge, Samuel Taylor, 1772-1834—Criticism and
interpretation. 2. Love in literature. I. Title.
PR4487.L65B37   1988
821'.7—dc19   88-4873
                        CIP

FOR KATE O'LEARY

Other books by the Author

The Symbolic Imagination: Coleridge and the Romantic Tradition. Princeton University Press, 1977.

Religious Perspectives in Faulkner's Fiction: Yoknapatawpha and Beyond. University of Notre Dame Press, 1972.

Coleridge and Christian Doctrine. Harvard University Press, 1969; Fordham University Press, 1987.

PREFACE

This book has grown, in true Coleridgean fashion, organically out of its predecessors. My first book on Coleridge, *Coleridge and Christian Doctrine,* had to do with his religious thought; the second, *The Symbolic Imagination: Coleridge and the Romantic Tradition,* extended the implications of his religious thought to his philosophy of symbol and to the use of symbolic language in his poetry, which draws much of its strength from the loving encounter of the poet with the world around him; *Coleridge and the Power of Love* explores both the human and the religious dimensions of love in his thought, his life, and especially his poetry.

There has been only one previous book-length study devoted to Coleridge and love, Anthony John Harding's fine book *Coleridge and the Idea of Love: Aspects of Relationship in Coleridge's Thought and Writing.* The philosophical richness of Harding's work, together with his application of Coleridge's ideas on relationship to morality and to social and political philosophy, has made it a permanently important source for Coleridge scholars. Although I have of course followed gratefully in Harding's wake, my own purpose is quite different. While Harding takes account of the poetry, it is not his primary concern; the present work, on the other hand, takes the poetry precisely as its central focus. This is above all a study of love as a "power"—a principle of action—in Coleridge's major poetry, set against the richly complex background of his philosophical and theological reflections on love and read in the context of his often troubled life.

The first chapter offers, in effect, Coleridge's "analytic" of love, drawn from his letters, his notebooks, and his philosophical and theological writings; it constitutes his ideal of what love should be. The second chapter turns to Coleridge's life and investigates the "shadow" side of this ideal: the actuality of his human relationships—his successes and his innumerable sad failures. These foundational chapters are followed by five chapters that study Coleridge's poetry in the light of his views on love and the limitations of love in his life. There are three kinds or "levels" of readings offered of the poetry. First, there is a reading (Chapter 3) of the six poems commonly called "conversation poems," which—while making no claim to completeness—reveals a pattern in each of these poems by which love acts as a "power" or "principle of action." Second, there are full and detailed readings (Chapters 4–6) of three central poems that reveal a similar role for love as a principle of action—poems chosen because of their special importance in the canon of Coleridge's poetry and in his life: "The Rime of the Ancient Mariner," "Christabel," and "Dejection: An Ode." Finally, in the last chapter, a group of later poems is discussed—"Constancy to an Ideal Object" in detail (as the only major poem among them), the others more cursorily—to show Coleridge's abiding concern with love and his ambivalent attitude toward it in his later life.

For the Coleridge specialist, it is hoped there is enough that is new in the readings of individual poems to bring fresh light or at least to raise new questions. However, for the nonspecialist Romantic scholar and the general reader of Coleridge, traditional interpretations are also reflected, especially in the chapters on the conversation poems and the

"Ancient Mariner." The chapters on "Christabel" and "Dejection" are more radically new approaches.

What is most important, however, is that throughout the poetry the thesis of Chapter 3 will be traced: on love as a "power." For this, Coleridge's distinction between *natura naturata* (nature as an effect, the "aggregate of phenomena") and *natura naturans* (nature as process, including the very source of power) will be of central importance; it is in effect, we shall see, the difference between the "spring of love" and the "burning fountain."

*   *   *

Along with dedicating it, one of the pleasantest chores involved in bringing a book to fruition is that of acknowledging the help of friends and colleagues. My own debts are many and varied.

First of all, I must thank the staffs of two libraries that have been particularly helpful: the Ellis Library of the University of Missouri–Columbia and the Thomas P. O'Neill Library of Boston College. I am grateful for the kindness and the efficiency of both.

I am pleased to thank the administration of the University of Missouri–Columbia, and especially the Department of English, for making possible a year's research leave in 1983–1984, during which much of the groundwork for this book was laid.

Chapter 1 of this work originally appeared in *Studies in Romanticism* (Spring 1985), and Chapter 6 in *Coleridge's Imagination: Essays in Memory of Pete Laver,* ed. Richard Gravil, Lucy Newlyn, and Nicholas Roe (Cambridge University Press, 1985); the discussion of "Constancy to an Ideal Object" in Chapter 7 appeared in an earlier version in *The Wordsworth Circle* (Spring 1983). I am grateful to the respective editors for their kind permission to use this material here.

During the course of work on this book, I have had the skillful and dedicated help of three research assistants, to whom I am very grateful: Jeff Johnson and A. J. Caschetta assisted me very ably at the University of Missouri–Columbia; and Thomas Lloyd of Boston College left a very special mark on the manuscript, not only by his diligent work and his sharp eye for detail but also because of the perceptive insight he brought to the Coleridge material.

To my secretary at Boston College, Margaret Tucker, I am deeply grateful, both for her remarkable efficiency and for her pleasant and gracious presence. To Marilynn Keil, senior departmental secretary of the English department at the University of Missouri–Columbia, I am indebted for consistently excellent logistical support and for innumerable kindnesses.

My debts to my Romantic colleagues are considerable, and it is a pleasure to acknowledge and record them here. First of all, several chapters of the book were originally delivered as lectures at the annual Wordsworth Conference in Grasmere, England. For the support and the stimulating discussion provided by that remarkable annual convocation of Romantic scholars I am deeply grateful. All of us who regularly attend the Conference owe much to the vigorous leadership of Richard and Sylvia Wordsworth and of Jonathan Wordsworth. I am especially grateful, too, for Coleridgean discussions over the years with—among many others—John Beer, David Erdman, Anthony Harding, Molly Lefebure, Thomas McFarland, W. J. B. Owen, Anya Taylor, and Jeanie Watson. I could hardly do better than hope that something of the spirit of the Conference has touched this work.

I am particularly thankful to Professor Kathleen Coburn, who graciously made available much of her own Coleridge material and the holdings of the Coleridge Room in the Victoria College Library of the University of Toronto. Along with all Coleridgeans, I am deeply in her debt as well for her magisterial editing of the Notebooks and for her faithful shepherding of the *Collected Coleridge*.

I owe very special thanks to Professors Philip C. Rule, S.J., of Holy Cross College and Howard Hinkel of the University of Missouri–Columbia, who read individual chapters of my work in progress and give me the benefit of their incisive criticism, and especially to Professor John L. Mahoney of Boston College, who read much of the manuscript at a late stage and helped me to sharpen and deepen my thought. My debts of friendship to these three Romantic colleagues are also considerable.

The completion of this book took place during my tenure as Thomas I. Gasson Professor of English at Boston College, 1985–1986, and my debts to that remarkable academic community are many: to the Jesuit Community of Boston College for its foresight in establishing the Gasson Chair; to the English department, under the chairmanship of Dennis Taylor, for its warm and collegial support; to the Jesuits of Roberts House, who made me so much at home among them; and to the splendid graduate students in my Coleridge seminar, whose enthusiasm and love for Coleridge soon came to match my own.

To Professors Walter Jackson Bate and David Perkins of Harvard University, who first introduced me to the serious study of Coleridge many years ago, I continue to be grateful, both for their friendship and for their continued encouragement.

Finally, to my colleagues in the English department at the University of Missouri–Columbia, who suffered through my chairmanship with me when these ideas were first brewing, as well as through a time of illness, I am grateful for their support and faithful friendship.

J.R.B.
Chestnut Hill, Massachusetts
Trinity Sunday, May 25, 1986

CONTENTS

Aids	*Aids to Reflection,* ed. H. N. Coleridge, *Complete Works* (Shedd), vol. 1
BL	*Biographia Literaria,* ed. Engell and Bate, *Collected Works,* vol. 7
CL	*Collected Letters,* ed. Griggs
CM	*Marginalia,* ed. Whalley, *Collected Works,* vol. 12
CN	*Notebooks,* ed. Coburn
FR	*The Friend,* ed. Rooke, *Collected Works,* vol. 4
LR	*Literary Remains,* ed. H. N. Coleridge, *Complete Works* (Shedd), vol. 5
LS	*Lay Sermons,* ed. White, *Collected Works,* vol. 6
PL	*Philosophical Lectures,* ed. Coburn
PW	*Complete Poetical Works,* ed. E. H. Coleridge
SC	*Shakespearean Criticism,* ed. Raysor
TT	*Specimens of the Table Talk,* ed. H. N. Coleridge, *Complete Works* (Shedd), vol. 6

Full citations for these works will be found in Works Cited at the end of this book.

Finally, Love is Love—essentially the same, whether the Object be a helpless Infant, our Wife or Husband, or God himself—Hence I say, that Love does not fly from us.

—*Notebooks, 1826*

CHAPTER 1

Coleridge's Ideal of Love

There is no concern of the Romantic poets more important than love. They are, to be sure, poets of revolution, poets of nature, poets of the feelings, whether simple or exalted. There are, in fact, almost as many romanticisms as one can discriminate. But central to all of them in one way or another, I suggest, is a preoccupation with love—whether of mankind, of nature, or of art. It is love that makes possible that "connectedness" (to use a word M. H. Abrams uses of Wordsworth)[1] that is the goal not only of Wordsworth but of all the Romantics, and it is the failure of love that is the greatest obstacle to this connectedness.

In Blake, from the "dark secret love" of the sick rose[2] to the exalted figure of Luvah, love and hate, union and separation, are at the heart of his vision. It was not for nothing that Luvah was "put for dung on the ground," but that the harvest might be plentiful.[3]

For Wordsworth, there is the simplicity of that "Maid whom there were none to praise / And very few to love"—but she is loved indeed, even after "she is in her grave."[4] There are, too, the "beauteous forms" of the Wye Valley that moved the poet to a "far deeper zeal / Of holier love."[5] And always there is this Wordsworthian principle:

> By love subsists
> All lasting grandeur, by pervading love;
> That gone, we are as dust.[6]

Keats was certain, we recall, "of nothing but of the holiness of the Heart's affections

---

1. *Natural Supernaturalism: Tradition and Revolution in Romantic Literature,* p. 295. Abrams goes so far as to equate connectedness and love in Wordsworth: "The sovereign function of poetry for Wordsworth is to sustain and propagate connectedness, which is love."

2. "The Sick Rose," *Songs of Experience,* in *The Complete Poetry and Prose of William Blake,* ed. David V. Erdman.

3. *The Four Zoas,* "Night the Ninth," in ibid.

4. "She Dwelt among the Untrodden Ways," *The Poetical Works of William Wordsworth,* ed. Ernest de Selincourt and Helen Darbishire, 2:30. Except for *The Prelude,* this will be the text used throughout for Wordsworth's poetry.

5. "Lines Composed a Few Miles above Tintern Abbey," lines 154–55, in *Poetical Works,* 2:259.

6. *The Prelude,* ed. Jonathan Wordsworth et al., 14. 168–70 (1850 version).

and the truth of Imagination"[7]—but of that he was certain indeed. He plumbed constantly the "Heart's affections"—tentatively and at times sentimentally in *Endymion,* mysteriously but more surefootedly in *Lamia* and "The Eve of St. Agnes," and more deeply in the great odes—exploring love of beauty, the love depicted in ancient art, and even the love of Cupid and Psyche themselves. In his last, unfinished masterpiece, *The Fall of Hyperion,* the poet finds that he himself must become a lover of humanity, one "to whom the miseries of the world / Are misery."[8] It is only because he loves humanity—not, to be sure, like the great humanitarians, whose love is complete, but enough to share its suffering—that he can become a true artist. There is no poetry without love.

For Shelley, love is the principle of all human life; it is "the bond and the sanction which connects not only man with man but with everything which exists."[9] We are not surprised, therefore, to follow the wanderings of *Alastor* as the poet searches for his visionary beloved, "obedient to the light / That shone within his soul";[10] or to find the same elusive vision in "The Sensitive Plant" and *Epipsychidion.* It is in the logic of Shelley's philosophy that the response to the fallen and fragmented world in *Prometheus Unbound* should be the loving reunion of Prometheus and Asia. As Prometheus says, "Most vain all hope but love."[11]

Even Byron, however cynical or world-weary he may be, still longs for love. Childe Harold is, after all, "the child of love,—though born in bitterness."[12] Manfred, even as he mourns the sinful love he has lost and cuts himself off deliberately from all needs or affections, human or divine, reaches out at the end for the touch of human sympathy, as he says to the old Abbot: "Give me thy hand."[13] The great *Don Juan* itself, for all its cynicism, remains a celebration of the possibilities as well as the limitations of love; even if love be seen there as more problem than probability, it remains Juan's—and Byron's—major concern.

M. H. Abrams has suggested that, for all the differences, there is a common denominator in Romantic love. "In the broad Romantic application of the term 'love,'" he notes, "as in recent depth-psychology, all modes of human attraction are conceived as one in kind, different only in object and degree, in a range which includes the relations of lover to beloved, children to parents, brother to sister, friend to friend, and individual to humanity," as well as, he adds, "of man to nature." However, although the Romantic poets agree in using the word *love* for the whole range of human relationships, Abrams says, "they differ markedly in their choice of the specific type of relationship which serves as the paradigm for all the other types." Wordsworth's "favored model," for example, is maternal love, "and the development of relationship in *The Prelude* is from the babe in his mother's arms to the all-inclusive

---

7. Letter to Benjamin Bailey (22 November 1817), in *The Letters of John Keats, 1814–1821,* ed. Hyder E. Rollins, 1:184.

8. *The Fall of Hyperion,* 1. 148–49, in *The Poems of John Keats,* ed. Jack Stillinger.

9. "Essay on Love," in *Shelley's Prose,* ed. David Lee Clark, p. 170.

10. *Alastor,* lines 492–493, in *Shelley's Poetry and Prose,* ed. Donald H. Reiman and Sharon B. Powers.

11. *Prometheus Unbound,* 1. 808, in ibid.

12. *Childe Harold's Pilgrimage,* 3, line 1094, in *The Complete Poetical Works,* ed. Jerome J. McGann, vol. 2.

13. *Manfred,* 3. 4. 149, in *The Selected Poetry of Lord Byron,* ed. Leslie A. Marchand.

'love more intellectual'"; Shelley's is sexual love, so that "all types of human and extrahuman attraction—all forces that hold the physical, mental, moral, and social universe together"—are represented by "categories which are patently derived from erotic attraction and sexual union"; Coleridge's paradigm is friendship, and he represents "sexual love as an especially intense kind of confraternity."[14]

However ironic it may seem in light of some of Coleridge's real-life failures in friendship—for example, his ruptured relationship with Wordsworth—it is beyond question that friendship held a privileged place in Coleridge's spectrum of relationships. As he wrote in 1796 to Thomas Poole, who was to remain a lifelong friend, "The Heart, thoroughly penetrated with the flame of virtuous Friendship, is in a state of glory."[15] Whether or not friendship was the paradigm for all the rest of his relationships is a question we shall leave open for the moment, while we turn to analyze Coleridge's general attitude toward love: his belief in the instinctive nature of love, his sense of its essential oneness, and his affirmation of love as a completion of one's self.

* * *

It is clear from Coleridge's reflections on love throughout his life that love is, or should be, an instinctive movement of our nature. Commenting on two lines of Wordsworth's "Immortality" ode ("As if their whole vocation / Were endless imitation"), Coleridge wrote: "The first lesson, that innocent Childhood affords me, is— that it is an instinct of my nature to pass out of myself, and to exist in the form of others."[16]

The importance of this impulse for love is explored more philosophically in a remarkable and very complex series of reflections on Kant in one of Coleridge's early notebooks.[17] He is commenting on Kant's *Foundation of a Metaphysics of Morals* (1785), in particular on the relationship and relative priority of duty and instinct. Coleridge finds much to admire in Kant, notably that (in Coleridge's translation) "it is not enough that we act in conformity to the Law of moral Reason—we must likewise FOR THE SAKE of that law." But Coleridge goes even further, adding, "It must not only be our Guide, but likewise our Impulse—Like a strong current, it must make a visible Road on the Sea, & drive us along that road."

The "duty" espoused by Kant is admirable, Coleridge feels, but even more admirable is the achieving of an impulse of sympathy. For "will not a pure will generate a feeling of Sympathy / Does even the sense of Duty rest satisfied with mere *Actions,* in the vulgar sense, does it not demand, & therefore may produce, Sympathy itself as an action?" In other words, will not the performance of good actions move one beyond mere duty to one's own moral nature to a more outward-looking sense of sympathy with the one for whom the good action is performed? On this, Kant is inadequate,

14. *Natural Supernaturalism,* p. 297.

15. *CL,* 1:235 (24 September 1796).

16. Notebook 47, ff. 20–20v (19 October 1830). The still unpublished notebooks quoted, unless otherwise indicated, are in the British Library.

17. *CN,* 1:1705 (December 1803).

Coleridge believes, and "very unfairly explains away the word Love into Beneficence." Coleridge is here much closer to Schiller than to Kant, as Kathleen Coburn has pointed out, for both Coleridge and Schiller contrast "the lesser morality of the iso- lated moral act *à contre-coeur* with the higher morality of the 'spontaneous', outflowing activity of a truly moral being."[18]

Coleridge never lost this conviction of the priority of the instinctive movement of the heart over the reasoned or carefully chosen act. In a notebook reflection written thirty years after his comments on Kant he says: "The more consciousness in Thoughts and Words, and the less in our impulses and general actions the better, and more healthful the state of both head and heart. As the flowers on an Orange Tree, in its time of blossoming, that burgeon forth, expand, fall, and are momently replaced, such is the sequence of hourly and momently charities in a pure and gracious Soul." Love not only is, but should be, in some sense "blind": "There is a sweet and holy Blindness in Christian *Love,* even as there is a blindness of Life, yea, and of Genius too, in the moment of productive energy."[19]

Let me make it clear, however, that this "spontaneity," this impulse for sympathy and love, is not for Coleridge simply a characteristic given at birth. The basic instinct for love is given, but—like a seed—it must be nurtured. Coleridge's sense of its growth is bound up with his profoundly Augustinian view of the human will. We are born, Coleridge argues, with a "responsible will"; we must work to make it a "free will." We are free only when we act according to what is best in our human nature, that is, when we make good choices. If we consistently choose the good, we generate a habit of virtue, so that in time we begin to move instinctively—as the saint does—in the direction of good, without need for the agony of decision.[20] So it is with love, which is of course an act of the will. By making loving decisions and acting on them, we gradually achieve a "habit of love," so that love becomes the instinct of our soul.

Coleridge never ceased to exalt such "movements of the heart." In 1805, he wrote of "the incalculable advantage of chiefly dwelling on the virtues of the Heart, of Habits of Feeling, & harmonious action, the music of the adjusted String at the impulse of the Breeze—and on the other hand the evils of books concerning particular actions, mi- nute case-of-conscience hair-splitting directions & decision."[21] In the last year of his life he still insisted that "motives are symptoms of weakness, and supplements for the deficient energy of the living *Principle.*"[22] That "living Principle" is, of course, the well of love springing up unbidden within the heart.

18. *CN,* 1:1705n. Coleridge's dissatisfaction with Kant was still evident years later: "I reject Kant's *stoic* principle, as false, unnatural, and even immoral, where in his Critik der Practischen Vernunft he treats the affections as indifferent . . . in ethics, and would persuade us that a man who disliking, and without any feeling of Love for, Virtue yet *acted* virtuously, because and only because it was his *Duty,* is more worthy of our esteem, than the man whose *affections* were aidant to, and congruous with, his Con- science." *CL,* 4:791–792, to J. H. Green (13 December 1817).

19. Notebook Q, ff. 2–2v (ca. 1831). Notebook Q is in the Berg Collection of the New York Public Library and is used with permission. The dates 1833–1834 are commonly given for this notebook, but this paragraph was used in a slightly revised form for the second edition of *Aids to Reflection* in 1831.

20. For a discussion of this conception of the human will as it appears in Coleridge's work, see my *Coleridge and Christian Doctrine,* pp. 110–11.

21. *CN,* 2:2435 (February 1805).

22. Notebook Q, f. 2v.

* * *

If Coleridge believed in the instinctive nature of love, he also believed in its continuity, its essential oneness. Late in his life, Coleridge wrote to his nephew Henry Nelson Coleridge, "In every thing *Continuity* is the characteristic both Quality and Property of my Being."[23] Or again, in a letter to his friend Charles Aders: "It is a maxim with me, to make Life as continuous as possible."[24] This is hardly surprising from the author of the "Treatise on Method," which extols "the mind which has been accustomed to contemplate not *things* only, or for their own sake alone, but likewise and chiefly the *relations* of things,"[25] or indeed from the author of "Religious Musings," who had written almost thirty-five years earlier:

> 'Tis the sublime of man,
> Our noontide Majesty, to know ourselves
> Parts and proportions of one wondrous whole![26]

The poet who wrote in 1817 of "the one Life within us and abroad"[27] sought from the beginning of his life to the end to articulate the unity and continuity he was constantly discovering around him.

It is no wonder, then, that Coleridge always affirmed the essential oneness of love. Thus, for example, in a beautiful letter of sympathy to his friend Thomas Poole on the death of his mother (an especially poignant letter, if one remembers that Coleridge did not even attend his own mother's funeral), he is able to affirm the role of filial love in the broadening and deepening of one's entire affective life. Coleridge tells Poole that, as his grief passes, "there will abide in your Spirit a great & sacred accession to those solemn Remembrances and faithful Hopes, in which and by which the Almighty lays deep the foundations of our continuous Life, and distinguishes us from the Brutes, that perish." This new awakening "facilitates that grand business of our Existence— still further, & further still, to generalize our affections."[28] New love is not separate and discrete, but grows out of already existing love—an extension, as it were, of its power.

In another letter of condolence, this time to Charles Aders on the death of his mother, Coleridge wrote of the "*friable,* incohesive sort of existence that characterizes the mere man of the World, a fractional Life made up of successive moments, that neither blend nor modify each other—a life that is strictly symbolized in the thread of Sand thro' the orifice of the Hour-glass, in which the sequence of Grains only *counterfeits* a continuity, and appears a *line* only because the interspaces between the Points are too small to be sensible." Where, he asks, is the "Eternal" that can fill up the "interspaces," that can make "all exist in each"? It is Love—Love that like Flame can

23. *CL,* 6:729 (20 February 1828).
24. *CL,* 5:266 (3 January 1823).
25. *FR,* 1:451.
26. "Religious Musings," lines 126–28, in *PW,* vol. 1. All quotations from Coleridge's poetry, unless otherwise indicated, will be taken from this edition.
27. "The Eolian Harp," line 26.
28. *CL,* 2:758 (19 September 1801).

pass successively, from this to this, ever the same essentially and yet taking up into it's character the nature of the Object in which it finds it's sustenance. . . . Mean is the *conjugal* love which does not partake of the *sisterly* and tend to renew and re-animate the filial."[29] Thus no true love will be exclusive, in the sense that it stands in the way of loving others:

> Warmth of particular Friendship does not imply absorption. The nearer you approach the Sun, the more intense are his Rays—yet what distant corner of the System do they not cheer and vivify? The ardour of private Attachments makes Philanthropy a necessary *habit* of the Soul. . . . Philanthropy (and indeed every other Virtue) is a thing of *Concretion*—Some home-born Feeling is the *center* of the Ball, that, rolling on thro' Life collects and assimilates every congenial Affection.[30]

We find the same sentiment expressed three decades later: "Our best loves and solicitudes may be in excess, and assuredly are so when they are exclusively confined to one object, or so attached as to detract from the love & care due to others."[31] Love is, of its very nature, not limiting but expansive.

If love is in this sense "organic"—growing into other forms by the very exercise of itself—then it follows that, as Coleridge wrote in one of his notebooks, "Love is always the same in essence; tho' it will receive a different shade according to its object. . . . Still, I say, that the Love of a Husband sitting by the sick bed of a beloved Wife, and that of a Brother by the bed of a dear Sister would differ only in *degree*. . . . Love is Sense of Union: and all its acts are tendencies to union, and ways of making ourselves conscious of the Same. Finally, Love is love—essentially the same, whether the Object be a helpless Infant, our Wife or Husband, or God himself."[32]

One further note should be added. Whatever the object of our love, in Coleridge's view it must be at once the same as ourselves and yet distinct from us; there must be, in other words, an "analogy" between us. First of all, "whatever is really & truly a part of our existing Nature, a universally existing part, may become an object of our love, & admiration."[33] Only then can there be a bond between us. On the other hand, "whatever forces us to contemplate or to feel an Object as *essentially* different from ourselves, and therefore incapable of Union, it with us or we with it, is proportionally detractive from Love."[34]

At the same time, the "other" must be allowed to keep its otherness. We recall that the first lesson Coleridge learned from "innocent childhood" (in his reflections on Wordsworth's "Immortality" ode) was that it was an instinct of his nature "to pass out of himself, and to exist in the form of others." The second lesson he learned was "not to suffer any one form to pass into *me* & to become a usurping *Self* in the disguise of what the German Pathologists call a *fixed Idea*"; for "this is always a *Self*-love—tho' the Conscience may be duped by the alterity & consequent distinct figurableness of the

---

29. *CL,* 5:266–67 (3 January 1823).
30. *CL,* 1:86, to Robert Southey (13 July 1794).
31. Notebook 47, ff. 21v-21 (19 October 1830).
32. Notebook F, ff. 55v-56v (November 1826).
33. *CN,* 2:2495 (March 1805).
34. Notebook F, f. 56v (November 1826).

form. As sure as it is cyclical, and forms the ruling *Eddy* in our mind, so surely does it become the representative of our Self, and = Self."[35] The continuity Coleridge always sought necessarily implies both sameness and difference, both unity and distinction. Without both, there will be not love, but either hatred or mere self-love.

* * *

Finally, love is for Coleridge a completion of ourselves and therefore implies—what we have already glanced at—a commonality between ourselves and the object of our love. A reflection of 1803 begins on what might seem a purely personal note: "My nature requires another Nature for its support, & reposes only in another from the necessary indigence of its Being.—Intensely similar, yet not the same; or may I venture to say, the same indeed, but dissimilar, as the same Breath sent with the same force, the same pauses, & with the same melody pre-imaged in the mind, into the Flute and the Clarion shall be the same Soul diversely incarnate."[36] However, the context makes it clear that he is speaking generally, even universally, for the very next notebook entry quotes approvingly from Plotinus that "all things desire that which is first from a necessity of Nature, prophesying as it were that they cannot subsist without the energies of that first Nature." Coleridge goes on to remark, "One participating in the same Root of Soul does yet spring up with excellences that I have not, to this I am driven, by a desire of Self-completion with a restless & inextinguishable Love."[37] Not long thereafter, and not surprisingly, we find him writing about Sara Hutchinson: "I love her as being capable of being glorified by me & as the means & instrument of my own glorification / In loving her thus I love two Souls as one, as compleat."[38]

Most of Coleridge's instances of "this instinctive Sense of Self-insufficingness" (as he calls it many years later),[39] are drawn from experiences of love between a man and a woman. In the same reflection of 1820, for example—in the wake, of course, of his own failure to be united with the woman of his longings—he wrote of "the Necessity in all men of human Sympathy, & hence in nobler Dispositions, the yearning after that full and perfect Sympathy with the *whole* of our Being which can be found only in a Person of the answering Sex to our own."[40] Yet in the same period we find him

35. Notebook 47, f. 20v (19 October 1830).
36. *CN*, 1:1679 (November 1803).
37. *CN*, 1:1680 (November 1803).
38. *CN*, 2:2530 (April 1805).
39. Notebook 60, f. 8 (October 1820).
40. Notebook 60, f. 7 (October 1820). See also Coleridge's comments on love in his discussion of *Romeo and Juliet*: "The individual has by this time learned the greatest and best lesson of the human mind—that in ourselves we are imperfect; and another truth, of the next, if not of equal, importance— that there exists a possibility of uniting two beings, each identified in their nature, but distinguished in their separate qualities, so that each should retain what distinguishes them, and at the same time each acquire the qualities of that being which is contradistinguished" (*SC*, 2:117–18).
Coleridge came to believe, too, what modern psychology has made a commonplace, that characteristics of the opposite sex are mingled in all of us. The following passage from a notebook entry of December 1829 is revealing:

N. B. By *feminine* qualities I mean nothing detractory—no participation of the *Effeminate*. In the best

writing much more generally of the experience of the union of love: "To make the Object one with us, we must become one with the Object—ergo, *an* Object.—Ergo: the Object must be itself a Subject—partially, a favorite dog—principally, a friend; wholly, *God*—the *Friend*—God is Love—i.e. an Object that is absolutely Subject . . . but a Subject that for ever condescends to become the *Object* for those that meet him subjectively."[41] Clearly, love of man and woman is, at least ideally, the most satisfying response on the human level to man's "instinctive Sense of Self-insufficingness," while only God—"the *Friend*," "Love" itself—can wholly fulfill it. But just as clearly other loves—of family, of friends—share in that work of self-completion. Such a view is implicit in this remarkable passage from a letter of 1822 to Thomas Allsop:

> I cannot love without esteem, neither can I esteem without loving. Hence I *love* but few—but those I love as my soul— for I feel that without them I should—not indeed cease to be kind, and effluent; but—by little and little become a soul-less fixed Star, receiving no rays nor influences into my being, a solitude, which I so tremble at that I cannot attribute it even to the Divine Nature.[42]

Those he loves, he loves "as his soul," as the missing parts of himself for which he searches. Without such "rays and influences" he would become "a solitude." Only in loving others can he be in any sense a whole self. "But for my conscience," he had written earlier, "i.e. my affections & duties toward others, I should have no Self—for Self is Definition; but all Boundary implies Neighbourhood—& is knowable only by Neighbourhood, or Relations."[43]

With these Coleridgean principles in mind, we can now turn to analyze Coleridge's ideal for each of the human relationships we call love: familial love, friendship, romantic love and passionate or sexual love, conjugal love, and love of God.

* * *

Anthony John Harding, in *Coleridge and the Idea of Love,* asks a question crucial to our reflections here: where, for Coleridge, "does consciousness begin?" "In awareness of another, or what we may call 'an I-Thou relationship,'" Harding replies.[44] He then

---

and greatest of men, most eminently—and less so, yet still present in all but such [?as are] below the average worth of Men, there is a feminine Ingredient.—There is the *Woman* in the Man— tho' not *perhaps the* Man in the Woman—Adam *therefore* loved *Eve*—and it is the Feminine in us even now that makes every Adam love his Eve, and crave for an Eve—

Why, I have inserted the dubious "perhaps"—why, it should be less accordant with truth to say, that in every good Woman there is *the Man* as an Under-song, than to say that in every true and manly Man there is a translucent Under-tint of the Woman—would furnish matter for a very interesting little Essay on sexual psychology. At present, it is enough to say, that the Woman is to look up to the *Man*, not in herself but out of herself. The Man looks out of himself for the realization and totalization of that in himself, which in himself dare not be totalized or permitted to be on the surface. (Notebook 42, ff. 63–63v)

41. Notebook 21 ½, f. 50 (1819–1820).
42. *CL,* 5:240 (29 June 1822).
43. *CN,* 2:3231 (1807–1810).
44. *Coleridge and the Idea of Love: Aspects of Relationship in Coleridge's Thought and Writing,* p. 144.

adduces an interesting passage from a Coleridge letter of April 1818 (whose Latin I here translate): "Consciousness is the knowledge of myself and another in the same act of knowing. Therefore, self-consciousness is the act by which I know myself as if I were another. The Me in the objective case is clearly distinct from the Ego."[45] One might be reminded of the biblical injunction, "Whoever would save his life shall lose it" (Luke 9:24). It is only in knowing another that we can know ourselves; it is only in looking outward that we can look inward.

For Coleridge, it is clear that this process begins with the relationship of mother and child, that all other relationships—human and divine—take their psychological origin from this primordial love. In a chapter of his Opus Maximum manuscript called "The Origin of the Idea of God," Coleridge wrote:

> Why have men a faith in God? There is but one answer. The man and the man alone has a Father and a Mother. The first dawnings of [the infant's] humanity will break forth in the eye that connects the mother's face with the warmth of the mother's bosom. . . . Ere yet a conscious self exists the love begins, and the first love is love to an other. Beyond the beasts, yea and above the nature of which they are inmates, man possesses love and faith and the sense of the permanent.

This is the beginning of the lifelong search for the fullness of love—the permanent. For only man, Coleridge goes on, is "irradiated by a higher power, the power namely of seeking what it can nowhere behold."[46]

The role of the father is less clearly defined, tending—no doubt because of Coleridge's own sad experience with his children—to take the form of anxiety for his offspring. As Coleridge wrote late in his life, "Many a Father can say, that it was since he had become a serious Christian that he first knew what it was to be verily and indeed concerned for a Son—what the *wrestling* of Love was."[47] Indeed, "a Father's Affection could not exist exempt from a Father's Anxiety."[48] The place of the mother remains for Coleridge unique and almost mystical; as he wrote to Thomas Allsop, "There is a religion in all deep love, but the Love of a Mother is, at your age, the veil of softer Light between the Heart and the heavenly Father!"[49]—but the role of the father is, by and large, to watch and wait in loving anxiety. He can advise but he cannot truly nourish or strengthen.[50] "A good Father speaks to us in nomine Dei; a Mother in

---

45. *CL*, 4:849, to Mr. Pryce (April 1818).
46. Quoted by J. H. Muirhead, *Coleridge as Philosopher*, pp. 252–53.
47. Notebook 36, f. 20v (Late 1827).
48. *CL*, 5:252, to Thomas Allsop (8 October 1822).
49. *CL*, 5:180 (20 October 1821).
50. This is nicely illustrated by a touching letter Coleridge wrote to his son Derwent, then seven years old: "For you are a big Thought, and take up a great deal of Room in your Father's Heart; and his Eyes are often full of Tears thro' his Love of you, and his Forehead wrinkled from the labor of his Brain, planning to make you good, and wise and happy. And your MOTHER has fed and cloathed and taught you, day after day, all your Life; and has passed many sleepless nights, watching and lulling you, when you were sick and helpless; and she gave *you* nourishment out of her own Breasts for so long a time . . . and she brought you into the world with shocking pains, and yet loved you the better for the Pains, which she suffered for you. . . . So it must needs be a horribly wicked Thing ever to forget, or wilfully to vex, a Father or a Mother: especially, a Mother. God is above all. . . . But after God's name, the name of Mother is the sweetest and most holy" (*CL*, 3:1–2 [7 February 1807]).

numine."[51] He can speak the word, but only she can give life.

As for sibling relationships, Coleridge has little or nothing to say about the relationships of brothers with brothers or sisters with sisters, but he speaks glowingly of brother-sister relationships. His most extended discussion is in a note of 1803 under the unpromising subject of incest.[52] He speaks there of "brotherly and sisterly love" as "strong Affection to one of the other sex, greatly modified by the differences of Sex, made more tender, graceful, soothing, consolatory, yet still remaining perfectly pure." The first great virtue of such relationships is that they are of such general occurrence that they are "a glorious fact *of* human Nature—the object therefore of religious Veneration to all that love their fellow-men or honor themselves."

The most important virtue of the brother-sister relationship, however, is in a sense propaedeutic: it helps prepare one not only for conjugal love but also for all the other relationships of life. First, it paves the way for married love: "By the long habitual practice of the sisterly affection preceding the conjugal, this latter is thereby rendered more pure, more even, & of greater constancy." Secondly, it prepares for a whole range of other affections: "To all this be added the beautiful Graduation of attachment, from Sister, Wife, Child, Uncle, Cousin, one of our blood, &c. on to mere Neighbour—to Townsman—to our Countrymen." We might note how once again, as so often, Coleridge emphasizes the continuity and therefore the essential unity of love.

It might be helpful to bear in mind that Coleridge's mother gave birth to ten children, nine boys and a girl. The only daughter, Ann, died during Coleridge's last years at Christ's Hospital. Since Coleridge's growing up took place surrounded by older brothers, his sister Ann may have been a momentary escape for him from the pressure of a very male-dominated environment. Hence it would be understandable if there were both observation and idealizing behind his thinking about the relationship of brother and sister.

* * *

Coleridge wrote and reflected perhaps as much on friendship as he did on any other human relationship, and his view of it was exalted. We have already seen his comment to his dear friend Thomas Poole that "The Heart, thoroughly penetrated with the flame of virtuous Friendship, is in a state of glory."[53] Considering that "glory" is an epithet used in the Old Testament to convey the presence of God, this is high praise indeed. And Coleridge's hopes for friendship are correspondingly high: "The unspeakable Comfort to a good man's mind . . . to have some one that understands one—& who does not feel, that on earth no one does. The Hope of this—always more or less disappointed, gives the *passion* to Friendship."[54] The note is typically Coleridgean: he is realistic about the fulfillment of the hope—as of course he had reason to

51. Notebook F, f. 97 (8 August 1827).
52. *CN,* 1:1637 (1803). Coleridge drew heavily on this notebook entry years later in preparing for his 1811 lecture on *Romeo and Juliet;* see *SC,* 2:116.
53. *CL,* 1:235 (24 September 1796).
54. *CN,* 1:1082.6 (December 1801–May 1802).

be—but the hope itself remains. The "passion" comes no doubt from the juxtaposition of hope and fear.

For Coleridge, friendship is never simply a "leap of the heart," however much he may give priority, here as everywhere, to the workings of the affections. Friendship must be founded on esteem. As he wrote to Humphry Davy: "But you know that I honor you, & that I love whom I honor. Love & Esteem with me have no dividual Being."[55] Many years later he wrote to Thomas Allsop: "I soon learnt to esteem you; and in esteeming, became attached to you."[56] Anthony Harding explains very convincingly some of the broader implications of the respective roles of emotion and moral judgment in human relationships, making it clear how Coleridge's views of friendship are bound up with his "belief in the interdependence of feeling and intellect which coloured almost every opinion Coleridge offered."[57]

The responsibilities of friendship are, of course, many: openness, sincerity, mutual concern, tolerance of one another's weaknesses. These themes recur throughout Coleridge's life and writings. Two such responsibilities, however, might be singled out. The first is the duty of friends to share their troubles with one another, resisting the temptation to spare one's friend the pain of knowing his suffering. In a particularly tender letter to Thomas Allsop (to whom many of his best reflections on friendship were written), Coleridge urges: "Whatever else may pass thro' your mind, never from any motive or with any view withhold from me your sorrows, your thoughts, or your feelings. . . . Send them onward to pass thro' mine—and between us both we shall be better able to give a good account of them!" The very act of sharing can be a healing. "Is there not a Dignity and a hidden *Healing* in the Suffering itself—which is soothed in the wish, and tempered in the endeavor of removing, or lessening, or supporting it in the soul of a dear friend?"[58]

But if the friend who suffers is called to share his pain and the duty of his friend is to listen with sympathy, there is also another responsibility, "the Duty of respecting the free-agency & individuality of your friend, or intimate."[59] Friends must, even as they long to share their friends' pain, also respect their privacy. "I know," Coleridge wrote (again to Allsop), "that there are inward withholdings that are as the attendant *Daimon* or Genius of an Individual, allotted to him together with his personëity." But even these will be listened to, "even tho' their utterances should be at times but a nervous singing in the ear."[60] Clearly friendship requires not only mutual concern and openness of heart but also tact and sensitivity.

However important the acts of friendship may be, even more important for Coleridge is the person. In an extended notebook reflection of 1803, written in the wake of a misunderstanding with Southey, Coleridge remarks on what "Prodigious Efficacy in preventing Quarrels and Interruptions of Friendship among Mankind in general, but

55. *CL*, 2:773 (31 October 1801).
56. *CL*, 5:164 (15 September 1821).
57. *Coleridge and the Idea of Love*, pp. 32–34; the quotation is from p. 33.
58. *CL*, 5:223 (16 March 1822). See also two other letters to Allsop: *CL*, 5:164 (15 September 1821) and 6:667 (1 February 1827).
59. *CL*, 6:531, to Mrs. Charles Aders (3 January 1826).
60. *CL*, 5:210 (9 February 1822).

especially among young warm-hearted men, would the habitual Reflection be, that the Almighty will judge us not by what we *do,* but by what we *are.*" He then asks himself why he became friends with Southey. "Because our pursuits were similar, our final aspirations similar; & because I saw plainly, that compared with the mass of men Southey was pure in his *Habits,* habitually indignant at oppression, *habitually* active in behalf of the oppressed, both by exertion & by self-sacrifice.—Not that he was Perfection; but because he was a far better man, than the vast majority of the young men, whom I knew." Coleridge wonders then about their quarrel: "What had I to oppose to all this?—An alteration of any of these *Habits?* Had Southey ceased to be Southey?— No. What then?—Why, one or two *Actions.*" If only the two friends had remembered in the midst of their quarrel the real basis of their friendship, all would have been well: "If either of us in some moment when from some accidental association a feeling of old Tenderness had revisited our Hearts, had paused—& asked our selves—Not what C. has *done?* or what has S. *done?*—but—Well! in spite of this—a bad business, to be sure—but spite of it—what *is* C. or S. on the whole?"[61]

This view of the priority of the person was to remain a lifelong conviction of Coleridge. In 1821 he wrote (again to Allsop):

> I soon learnt to esteem you; and in esteeming, became attached to you. I began by loving the man on account of his conduct, but I ended by valuing the actions chiefly as so many looks and attitudes of the same person. '*Hast* thou any thing? Share it with me, and I will pay thee an equivalent. *Art* thou any thing? O then we will exchange souls.'[62]

Again, in a letter of thanks to Allsop for a gift: "On the one Scale—I love you so truly, that in the first glance as it were and *well-come* of this pledge of your anxious affection it delights me for the very act's sake. I think only of it and you—or rather both are one and the same, and I live in you as the Agent."[63]

There is indeed an exchange of life between friends, so that each one takes on something of the being of the other: "Your Letter of this morning is not [to] be answered by *words.* There are acts of friendship where it is better not to give birth even to the whole of the inward *feelings* appropriate to them / what does not pass forth, remains within, and it's own stillness sinks more securely into us, & becomes one with our habitual Being."[64]

*   *   *

Coleridge's discussions of romantic love (which he sometimes refers to as "being in love") frequently lead to reflections on the relationship between love and sexual desire. The role of sexuality in love is often misunderstood, he believes, because of a failure to distinguish between desire and lust. Wordsworth, for example, Coleridge says,

---

61. *CN,* 1:1605 (October 1803). There is a similar reflection in a letter to Thomas Poole of 22 August 1796; *CL,* 1:230–31.
62. *CL,* 5:164 (15 September 1821).
63. *CL,* 5:176 (24 September 1821).
64. *CL,* 2:1177, to Daniel Stuart (22 August 1806).

"ridicules the existence of any other passion, than a compound of Lust with Esteem & Friendship, confined to one Object, first by accidents of Association, and permanently, by the force of Habit & a sense of Duty."[65] Of this view Coleridge says: "Now this will do very well—it will suffice to make a good Husband . . . but still it is not *Love*."[66] Coleridge did not remain even this indulgent toward what he had characterized—perhaps caricatured—as Wordsworth's view, for a decade later we find him snorting: " 'Love a vehement appetite for an Object which is at the same time *esteemed!*' *Appetite* for a *Person*! *Esteem* for a Thing! Absurd incongruities!"[67]

What then *is* romantic love, if it is not "a compound of Lust with Esteem & Friendship, confined to one Object"? Coleridge replies that it is the "exclusive sexual Attachment, such as may exist in the best & noblest conditions of human nature—*that attachment* of a refined & honorably honest Man, which is *exclusively* felt to some *one* Woman; & vice versa, that of a Woman to some one Man." Such an attachment springs from the "instinctive sense of Self-insufficingness" that is common to all—and that, as we have seen, is for Coleridge at the root of all love. "In a pure & noble mind," he goes on, "the sense of its Self-insufficingness, the sense that it is of itself *homo dimidiatus*, but *half* of a compleat Being, exists *consciously*, & with *reflection*." But, Coleridge insists, this sense of incompleteness "is extended to the *whole* of his complex Nature, to the Understanding, to the Affections, as well as to its animal organization."[68]

Thus arises the question so often canvassed by Coleridge of the relationship between love and desire or love and lust. Coleridge distinguished implicitly, and sometimes explicitly, between lust and desire. For example, in a comment on the early chapters of Genesis, Coleridge makes it clear why lust is inferior to desire. "The mere *sensations* that accompany *Lust*, may exist, yet *Love* alone be the object of consciousness—It is only, when these sensations are the direct object of consciousness, and desired for themselves, that Lust obtains a Being. It is no longer cloathed & hidden in a loftier Nature, & taken up into the Humanity."[69] True desire, "cloathed & hidden in a loftier Nature," can only be found in company with love—which is of course that "loftier Nature."

Desire comes into being, Coleridge believes, out of fear of change or loss. One who has "truly and intensely loved a lovely and beautiful Woman" must have felt "that it is the disquieting sense of Change, the thought-flash, 'I shall lose her, perhaps,' that awakes DESIRE!" It is this "that prompts him to press the Beloved Object closer to himself, as if to inclose it in his own Life, and to confound it with his Being, thus sacrificing in order to secure it!"[70]

65. This characterization of Wordsworth's view immediately follows Coleridge's famous comment, "Wordsworth is by nature incapable of being in Love, tho' no man more tenderly attached."
66. *CL,* 3:305, to Henry Crabb Robinson (12 March 1811).
67. Notebook 20, ff. 44–43v (1821–1823).
68. Notebook 60, ff. 9v-10 (October 1820).
69. Notebook 42, ff. 20v-21 (November 1829). On love and lust or love and concupiscence, see also *CL,* 3:305, to Henry Crabb Robinson (12 March 1811); Notebook 20, ff. 44–43 (1821–1823); Notebook 44, ff. 12v-13 (1830); Notebook 48, ff. 8–9 (November 1830); and Notebook Q, ff. 56v-57 (1833–1834).
70. Notebook 26, f. 3 (c. 7 May 1826).

Such love happens, too, in a moment of time, however long it may have been in preparation. "I believe," Coleridge wrote,

> that *Love* (as distinguished both from Lust and from that habitual attachment which may include many Objects, diversifying itself by *degrees* only), that that *Feeling* (or whatever it may be more aptly called), that specific mode of Being, which one Object only can possess, & possesses totally, is always the abrupt creation of a moment—tho' years of *Dawning* may have preceded.[71]

One summary view of romantic love is wonderfully reminiscent of Coleridge's description of the workings of imagination in the *Biographia Literaria:* "The poet, described in *ideal* perfection, brings the whole soul of man into activity, with the subordination of its faculties to each other, according to their relative worth and dignity."[72] In a long notebook entry of 1820, Coleridge describes love as "a co-alescence of all our Powers & Receptivities, to one particular Object." This coalescence with a beloved object is "the result of a secret Intuition of a Sympathy in its Being with our own." It must aim at a complete union, involving every level of one's being, for "unless the Head, the Heart, & the Body concentrate their separate desires of perfecting them selves by union, the Head with the Head, the Heart with the Heart, the Person with the Person, to one Individual, it is not *Love,*—for Love is a Passion of the whole Being in harmony."[73]

The parallel with the working of imagination is perhaps not merely fanciful. Both poetry and love are for Coleridge participations in the eternal life of God, both aim at the most intense kind of unity, both "bring the whole soul of man into activity," and both are capable of giving the deepest joy. As drama critic Jack Kroll has remarked, perhaps art and love are "two forms of the same energy."[74]

*   *   *

Coleridge's views on marriage manifest more development throughout his life than those on any other human relationship. In his salad days as a young radical, Coleridge tended to emphasize strongly, if not exclusively, the societal dimension of marriage. "*Permanent* cohabitation," he wrote to John Thelwall, is "useful to Society as the best conceivable means . . . of ensuring nurture & systematic education to infants & children."[75] On such nurture and education depends the future of society. Equally important for society, however, is the moral growth of the individual, and to this end marriage is essential. In one of his *Conciones ad Populum* of 1795 Coleridge spoke glowingly of the crucial role of the "domestic affections" in building up society.

> The happiness of Mankind is the *end* of Virtue, and Truth is the Knowledge of the *means;* which he will never seriously attempt to discover, who has not habitually interested himself

---

71. *CL,* 3:304, to Henry Crabb Robinson (12 March 1811).
72. *BL,* 2:15–16.
73. Notebook 60, ff. 14–14v (October 1820).
74. "Sondheim Paints a Picture," *Newsweek,* 14 May 1984, p. 84.
75. *CL,* 1:306 (6 February 1797).

in the welfare of others. The searcher after Truth must love and be beloved; for general Benevolence is a necessary motive to constancy of pursuit; and this general Benevolence is begotten and rendered permanent by social and domestic affections. Let us beware of that proud Philosophy, which affects to inculcate Philanthropy while it denounces every home-born feeling, by which it is produced and nurtured. The paternal and filial duties discipline the Heart and prepare it for the love of all Mankind. The intensity of private attachments encourages, not prevents, universal Benevolence.[76]

However much Coleridge might have been influenced by Godwin, clearly he did not follow him in his disdain for marriage. As Anthony Harding says, "Coleridge indeed held with Burke that family loyalty, so far from being incompatible with loyalty to the state, was the root from which national loyalty should grow."[77]

As time went on—and without ever foregoing his belief that the institution of marriage was the linchpin of civilization—Coleridge came to stress more and more the importance of marriage (as Harding puts it) "for the more personal reason that it answered the need for growth and fulfilment of the individual mind."[78] But it was not, one might add, merely the growth of the individual mind that was at issue for Coleridge; it was the growth of the whole self. More and more did Coleridge, writing no doubt out of his own solitude on this deepest level, come to write of his sense of the individual as incomplete, needing the fulfillment of another self. "Every human Individual, sit Vir, sit Femina, HOMO DIMIDIATUS est: and Love is the Yearning of the *whole* Person after a union with that, which is felt necessary to it's completion."[79] In 1826 he wrote that marriage is a "*Moral* Union, in which each of the two Persons morally perfects the other. Dimidia in totum concurrunt, like two opposite Mirrors, each containing the image of the other."[80] Again, in 1827, he pictured the two parties to a marriage as "each seeking in the other the completing Counterpart of its *total* Being."[81]

From here it is but the shortest of steps to the realization that the ideal marriage is the highest form of friendship, and indeed that friendship can reach its perfection only in marriage. This notion, which was to recur frequently throughout the rest of Coleridge's life, began to appear around 1810, the year of the rupture of Coleridge's friendship with Wordsworth. Writing in his copy of Sir Thomas Browne's *Religio Medici*, Coleridge took issue with Browne, who had written: "I never yet cast a true affection on a woman, but I have loved my friend as I do vertue, my soul, my God." Coleridge replied:

Friendship satisfies the *highest* parts of our nature; but a wife, who is capable of friendship, satisfies *all*. The great business of real unostentatious Virtue is—not to eradicate any genuine instinct or appetite of human nature; but—to establish a concord and unity betwixt all

76. *Lectures 1795: On Politics and Religion,* ed. Lewis Patton and Peter Mann, in *Collected Works,* ed. Coburn, pp. 45–46.
77. Harding, *Coleridge and the Idea of Love,* p. 22.
78. Ibid., p. 106.
79. *CL,* 4:914, to C. A. Tulk (26 January 1819).
80. Notebook F, f. 37v (1–10 April 1826).
81. Notebook 48, ff. 4v-5 (6 November 1830).

parts of our nature, to give a Feeling & a Passion to our purer Intellect, and to intellectualize our feelings & passions. This a happy marriage, blessed with children, effectuates, in the highest degree, of which our nature is capable.[82]

Years later Coleridge wrote, "Herein does Friendship differ from Love, that it is not (or in the case of man and man), cannot be, a union of the *whole* Being—*Perfect* Friendship is only possible between Man and Wife," adding—"even as *there* is to be found the bitterest enmity."[83]

Coleridge's two emphases in marriage, the societal and the personal, come together meaningfully and profoundly in his view of the sacramental nature of marriage. He soon set aside his early rejection of marriage as a sacramental rite ("spells uttered by conjurors"),[84] and for the rest of his life fairly consistently viewed marriage as a sacrament, having therefore both a personal and an ecclesial dimension. In *Aids to Reflection* (1825) he wrote: "It might be a mean [*sic*] of preventing many unhappy marriages, if the youth of both sexes had it early impressed on their minds, that marriage contracted between Christians is a true and perfect symbol or mystery." For marriage is, he went on (alluding to Ephesians 5:22–23), "symbolical of the union of the soul with Christ the Mediator," and is therefore "perfectly a sacramental ordinance."[85]

From the very beginning, even before he came to see marriage as sacramental, Coleridge believed firmly in its indissolubility. One might say that his belief in the sacredness of marriage is as much tied to his views on the stability of "the idea of the State" as to his views of sacrament, for—as we have seen—he clearly considers marriage an essential stabilizing force in human society. One of his earliest expressions of the sacredness of the marriage bond, in fact, is in the course of a long letter to John Thelwall concerning Godwinian principles of society. It is in this context that he wrote quite simply—and directly in opposition to Godwin—"*Marriage is indissoluble.*"[86] As late as 1830 we find him writing: "The sanctity of the Marriage bond is the very basis & conditio sine qua non of all the other civil obligations & charities—at once the taproot, and the protecting, investing and reproducing Cortex, Liber and Alburnum of the whole Tree of Civilization."[87]

Although Coleridge insisted throughout his life on this societal dimension of marriage, there is evidence—not least of all his lifelong refusal to seek a divorce from Mrs. Coleridge—that his view of marriage as a religious commitment was at least as important to him. His comments on the Book of Deuteronomy late in his life are revealing on this point, for he there maintains that the Deuteronomic right to divorce was

---

82. *CM*, 1:751. George Whalley conjectures that this note may have been written about 1810.

83. *CL*, 4:904, to Unknown Correspondent (8 January 1819). See also *CL*, 4:914, to C. A. Tulk (26 January 1819).

84. *CL*, 1:306, to John Thelwall (6 February 1797).

85. *Aids*, p. 138n. See also *TT*, p. 349 (27 September 1830). A year after the publication of *Aids*, Coleridge had second thoughts about this view and retracted his comment in *Aids*; see Notebook F, f. 37v. However, in 1827 he returned to the earlier view, quoting St. Paul, who "so profoundly calls Marriage a great Mystery, or Sacramental Symbol" (Notebook 35, f. 41). For a fuller treatment of the sacramentality of marriage, see my *Coleridge and Christian Doctrine*, pp. 180–81 and n. 57.

86. *CL*, 1:213 (13 May 1796).

87. Notebook 43, f. 53v (16 May 1830).

permitted to the Israelites only "for the hardness of their hearts"—"on the same principle, on which with far doubtfuller necessity & expedience, the horrid Trade of Prostitution is tolerated in our Cities. But it was the *Law* that came by Moses: Truth and Grace by Jesus Christ."[88]

In his role as the sage of Highgate, Coleridge was occasionally asked to offer advice on marriage to prospective brides and grooms—and there is no evidence that he was ever conscious of the irony of the failed husband counseling those about to be married. To one young man, after insisting that he had "but little to say," Coleridge wrote six pages of "principles" for the choice of a spouse.[89] They may be taken as fairly typical of Coleridge's views. The first two principles emphasize the importance of the decision to be made; the man's happiness and therefore "his future usefulness and his own moral Being" depend on it. The third principle is the heart of the matter, outlining the characteristics to be sought for in a wife: "moral character and freedom from diseases"; "understanding so far proportionate to your own as to make her capable of being a judicious Friend, an occasional Adviser, & a fire-side Companion"; "*natural* sensibility, natural disposition to sympathy"; "steadiness of character" and "sense of Duty"; mutual suitability with oneself.

This last, mutual suitability, requires a word of explanation, for under this heading Coleridge suggests several important and revealing questions: "Does she *sincerely* adopt my opinions on all important subjects? Has she at least that known *docility* of nature which, uniting with true wifely love, will dispose her so to do? Do her notions of Happiness point to the same source as mine—or to Dress, Equipage, Visiting, a fine House &c? Am I sure that I really *love* her?" One is not surprised to find the insistence on true love, but it is rather disconcerting to find Coleridge, who sometimes spoke feelingly of the intellectual gifts of women, articulating such a complete intellectual subordination of wife to husband.[90]

The final principle is a very pragmatic exhortation for the young man to consult his own material interests in arranging his marriage, in particular not to endanger his own fortune—not for purely selfish ends but for the sake of the future use of his God-given powers and abilities.

---

88. Notebook 43, ff. 50v-51 (25 May 1830).

89. *CL*, 4:903-9, to an Unknown Correspondent (8 January 1819). See also *CL*, 6:793-95, to John Anster (July 1829), and 6:878-79, to James Gillman, Jr., and Susan Steel (10 January 1832). For earlier advice on marriage, see *CL*, 3:92-93, to Daniel Stuart (18 April 1808).

90. The story is perhaps not quite as simple as this. Coleridge was, to be sure, quite capable of being thoroughly conventional in his view of women, as when he remarked, "Women are infinitely fonder of clinging to and beating about, hanging upon & keeping up & reluctantly letting fall, any doleful or painful or unpleasant subject, than men of the same class & rank. . . . Is it want of generalizing power & even instinct?" (*CN*, 2:2310 [December 1804]). Or again: "Cunning is the poor substitute for Wisdom. Hence Women are *cunning*" (*CN*, 3:4270 [1815]). On the other hand, he wrote to Southey of his esteem for the intelligence of Mary Evans, the first great love of his life: "We formed each other's minds—our ideas were blended" (*CL*, 1:123 [3 November 1794]). Coleridge says of Mary Evans that she is "a young Lady, who beneath the soft surface of feminine delicacy possesses a mind acute by Nature, and strengthened by habits of Reflection" (*CL*, 1:51, to Mary Evans [7 February 1793]). It must be confessed, though, that Mary Evans is seen as the exception rather than the rule, for she is "possessed of a Mind and of a Heart above the usual Lot of Women" (*CL*, 1:131, to Mary Evans [Early November 1794]).

Coleridge's advice to a young woman is rather more general, though persuasive and often eloquent. She must marry someone whom she can *"conscientiously,* vow to love, *honor,* and *respect."* In other words, she must have "a *Soul*-mate as well as a *House-* or a *Yoke*-Mate!" She must choose a man free of hereditary disease and of a sufficiently strong constitution, lest she be left a young widow. Between them they should have "worldly means proportional to their former Rank and Habits." Finally, her prospective husband must be a man with a strong sense both of duty and of honor.[91] Admirable though these qualities may be, it is difficult to escape the impression that Coleridge's view of marriage is weighted in favor of the man, for it is he who is the intellectual leader. On this issue at least, Coleridge was clearly a man of his time.

Whatever its limitations, Coleridge's ideal of marriage was still a lofty one. In the very year of his own marriage he wrote to Southey: "Domestic Happiness is the greatest of things sublunary—and of things celestial it is perhaps impossible for unassisted Man to believe anything greater."[92] A whole lifetime later he still saw marriage as a matter of "transcendent importance, as a union for life, a union of will, mind and body, in weal and woe, in sickness and health, thro' good report and evil report—in short, a combination of two individuals of different sexes into one moral and spiritual Person."[93]

* * *

We began our survey of Coleridge's views on human relationships with the primordial relationship of mother and child. It is significant that Coleridge's most touching reflections on motherhood appear in the Opus Maximum chapter on "The Origin of the Idea of God." We now turn at last to that climactic relationship of love between man and God, whose "first dawnings" appeared in the instinctive love of the child for its mother.

That instinctive love of the child is already, Coleridge makes clear, implicitly a desire for God. As early as 1803, in a comment on a text of Plotinus, Coleridge wrote of how we are "driven, by a desire of Self-completion with a restless & inextinguishable Love." The object of this love is God, for he goes on: "God is not all things, for in this case he would be indigent of all; but all things are God, & eternally indigent of God."[94] Implicit here, as elsewhere in Coleridge, is a belief in "participation," by which man shares in the being of God and yet longs for fuller union with him. Some years later he wrote: "There is a capaciousness in every *living* Heart, which retains an aching Vacuum . . . God only can *fill* it."[95] Again, toward the end of his life, Coleridge expressed the same sense of union with God joined with longing for even deeper union: "awakening in myself the firm faith in his Presence I offer to him his own best gifts, the yearnings of my spirit after him, the Father of Spirits."[96]

91. *CL,* 5:152–58, to an Unknown Correspondent (June 1821).
92. *CL,* 1:158 (Early August 1795).
93. *CL,* 6:795, to James Gillman, Jr. (July 1829).
94. *CN,* 1:1680 (November 1803).
95. *CL,* 4:607, to Washington Allston (25 October 1815).
96. Notebook 42, ff. 38–38v (November 1829).

What is operating here is of course final causality, the innate principle in human nature by which God draws all mankind to himself—the same principle Augustine expresses in his famous "Inquietum est cor meum, Domine." Coleridge wrote in a letter to his nephew: "I adore the living and personal God, whose Power indeed is the *Ground* of all *Being,* even as his Will is the efficient, his Wisdom the instrumental, and his Love the final Cause, of all *Existence.*"[97] To love God is for Coleridge the ultimate aim of human life, for God "framed my heart to love him."[98] Such an aim is awesome, but natural to man: "To be one with God, the Father—an aweful thought beyond all utterance of the Awe which it inspires; but by no means wild or mystical. On the contrary, all our experience moves in this direction."[99] Coleridge sums it up in a wonderful flash of metaphor: "The needle trembles, indeed, and has its dips and declinations, but it is pointing to the right pole, or struggling to do so; and as long as God does not withdraw his polar influence, nor the soul its polar susceptibility, I must not dare withdraw *my* love."[100]

The human temptation as Coleridge sees it, often succumbed to in the history of Christianity, is to let fear supersede love in our relationship with God. Coleridge's own feelings in the matter are suggested by a story he recorded concerning Ivo, the thirteenth-century Bishop of Chartres, who met "a grave Matron" carrying fire in one hand and water in the other. When asked what she meant to do with them, she replied: "My purpose is with the fire to burn Paradise, & with my water to quench the flames of Hell, that men may serve God without the incentives of hope & fear, & purely from the love of God."[101] Such a rejection of purely prudential morality is typical of Coleridge's view throughout his life. "Selfish Prudence may be enlisted into the service of Morality . . . but it never, never can be the Leader or Guide. . . . Fear & Hope may have been the preparatives, the pioneers on the road; but we reach Christ only by the love of Christ."[102] "Unless that *Fear,* which is the *Beginning* of Wisdom, shall proceed to LOVE, there can be no Union with God: for God is Love."[103]

Something of the psychology, and perhaps the metaphysics, of the process is suggested by a notebook entry from the last year of Coleridge's life. "Love is the Apotheosis of *Fear;* but of a Fear that itself proceeds from Love. The creaturely Heart, contracting itself toward itself, & thus self-contrasted with the Divine Idea in its' essence, is religious *Fear;* which in its' rebound & expansion toward God becomes Love."[104] Fear is itself a gift of God, one that includes an implicit awareness of one's creaturely state. As the heart "contracts," it becomes more and more aware of its own

97. *CL,* 4:894, to William Hart Coleridge (8 December 1818).
98. Notebook 42, f. 38v (November 1829).
99. Notebook F, f. 75 (7 January 1830).
100. *CL,* 4:677, to Rest Fenner (22 September 1816).
101. *CN,* 1:872 (December 1800).
102. Notebook F, ff. 88–88v (Good Friday 1832). For Coleridge's strictures against the purely prudential morality of William Paley, whose *Principles of Moral and Political Philosophy* (1785) was used as a textbook at Cambridge for much of the nineteenth century, see *Lay Sermons,* ed. R. J. White, in *Collected Works,* ed. Coburn, pp. 186–87, Coleridge's note.
103. *CL,* 3:153, to Sir George Beaumont (30 December 1808).
104. Notebook Q, f. 13 (1833–1834).

littleness in comparison with God, which in turn prompts it to "rebound," reaching out toward God in a movement of love that acknowledges the greatness of God and the creature's loving dependence on him. Paradoxically, this acknowledgment of its own littleness allows the heart at the same time to "expand," as constricting fear turns to love.

Coleridge makes it clear, however, that this movement of the heart does not take place without the concurrence of the will. Proposing a discourse on the phrase "Thy Kingdom come" from the Lord's Prayer, Coleridge sets as his aim "to remove all mysticism & strangeness from this—to shew that unity with God implies no less but rather an *intension* of personal distinction,—to pourtray the World as it would be, if the Will of God were done on Earth *as* it is in Heaven—i.e. by a coincidence of the human with the divine Will, and not merely by an overawing of the Human Will by the Divine Power."[105] Because man is made in the image of God, the human will is meant to be a reflection of the Divine Will; sin—a failure of love—is in fact the refusal of the finite will to subordinate itself to the Absolute Will. It is only when the finite will can freely acknowledge its essential dependence on the Absolute Will that the union of love between man and God can take place. Such a union is the result not simply of a movement of the heart but of a commitment of the whole person, under the aegis of the will.[106]

Coleridge makes it abundantly clear, too, that the union of love between man and God is not effected solely in the private relationship of the soul with God in prayer, however important this may be. We must find God in each other—the child in the mother, the lover in the beloved, the friend in the friend, the husband in the wife and the wife in the husband. For "the best, the truly lovely, in each & all is God. Therefore the truly Beloved is the symbol of God to whomever it is truly beloved by!"[107] God is revealed in fact, in greater or less degree, by all his creation, for "all creaturely excellence is a shrine or more or less transparent veil, thro' which the divine Attributes reveal their presence."[108] It is in realizing the indwelling of God in all creation, especially in his people, that we become truly Christian, for it is only then that we truly find ourselves in others and God in all: "Our, we, us, are the Christian pronouns."[109] Love of God and love of man are not separate for Coleridge, but inextricably bound up with one another.

In the person of Christ, Coleridge sees the perfect image of God's love—and at the same time the epitome of all human love. This latter conception draws strength from "the Idea of the Son of God as the Son of Man, the indwelling ground and substance of our proper Humanity—the Idea of Christ, as the Divine Humanity." All Christians are indeed one with Christ, so that "every act of Christian love to the humblest Brother in whom the divine Humanity is awakened by faith in Christ, is done to Christ."[110] It is

105. Notebook 41, f. 64 (September 1829).
106. For an extended discussion of the relationship between the finite will and the Absolute Will, see my *Coleridge and Christian Doctrine*, pp. 108–12.
107. *CN*, 2:2540 (April 1805).
108. Notebook 47, f. 4 (1 October 1830).
109. Notebook 36, f. 21 (Late 1827).
110. Notebook 47, f. 3v (1 October 1830).

at the same time Christ who, as perfect image of the Father, shows us how to love: "by contemplating Glory we are glorified, & pass from Glory to Glory—that which we see, see that it is lovely, & seeing love, we gradually become. It is the *Love* of Christ not alien [?care] constitutes us Christians."[111] For God has "provided an access and return to himself for the poor self-lost Spirit in Christ the Mediator."[112]

Finally, God has given man, in the revelation of the Trinity, an image of perfect love. In the trinitarian life of the Godhead, love is identified with life itself. "Here Life is *Love,* communicative outpouring Love."[113] The three Divine Persons are in fact, in Coleridgean terminology, Ipseity (the Father), Alterity (the Son), and Community (the Spirit). "Community" is precisely the love between Father and Son, and the life they live is a "Life of Love, i.e. a Love which *is* Life, a Life which is wholly and essentially Love."[114]

*   *   *

Early in this chapter, we noted M. H. Abrams's observation that Coleridge's favored paradigm for love, against which all other relationships are measured, is friendship. Now, in the light of our consideration of Coleridge's views on a variety of relationships, perhaps Abrams's view can be qualified. I would like to suggest that Coleridge's preferred model is in fact "*married* friendship," for, as we have seen, it is only in marriage that friendship can come to its perfection. It is only in marriage that the longed-for union can take place on every level of one's being, including the physical: "Friendship satisfies the *highest* parts of our nature; but a wife, who is capable of friendship, satisfies *all*."[115]

Coleridge's "favored paradigm" can surely be useful in understanding and evaluating his ideas on other relationships, but there is another relationship that is equally important in understanding Coleridge's views on love—his "prime analogate," that is, that love which philosophically gives meaning to all the rest. For it will perhaps be clear by this time that implicit in all Coleridge's discussion of love is what we might call an "analogy of love." For Coleridge, all love—like all being—is "consubstantial," that is, it shares in the same reality, as God the Son is consubstantial with the Father, one yet distinctly other. Coleridge makes it clear—as I hope we have done here—that all love is ultimately one, so that love begets love, one form of love nourishing and

111. Notebook F, f. 88 (Good Friday 1832).
112. Notebook 46, f. 13 (September 1830).
113. Notebook 23, f. 26 (5 May 1827).
114. Notebook 37, ff. 35v-36 (14 March 1828). For a splendid articulation of Coleridge's views on the Trinity, written shortly after his affirmation of his return to Trinitarian Christianity (in Malta in 1805), see his letter to Thomas Clarkson (*CL,* 2:1195–96 [13 October 1806]). A letter of the same month to George Fricker traces the path he took from Unitarianism to Trinitarianism (*CL,* 2:1188–90 [9 October 1806]). The first statement of his return to Trinitarianism is found in *CN,* 2:2444 (February 1805). A full discussion of Coleridge's views on the Trinity may be found in my *Coleridge and Christian Doctrine,* chap. 4.
115. *CM,* 1:751.

strengthening another. Thus any form of love is "analogous" to any other, different yet deeply the same.

Any analogy that is based on the analogy of being, as is this analogy of love, implies a hierarchical structure. Without attempting to hierarchize all the relationships of which Coleridge wrote (I suspect he might have hierarchized them somewhat differently at different times in his life), we can surely concede that some such hierarchy is implicit throughout. For example, in a passage we have seen already, he offers a simple form of such a structure: "To make the Object one with us, we must become one with the Object . . . Ergo: The Object must be itself a Subject—partially a favorite dog—principally a friend; wholly, *God.*"[116]

In any such analogical structure there must be a "prime analogate," that being in which the perfection in question—being, truth, goodness, love—is contained in its fullness. There must be a "resting-place" for the mind as it considers the meaning of such perfections. Writing of married love, Coleridge says: "There is another Reason why Friendship is of somewhat less Value, than Love which includes Friendship—it is this—we may love many persons, all *very* dearly; but we cannot love many persons, all *equally* dearly. There will be *differences,* there will be *gradations*—our nature imperiously asks a *summit,* a *resting-place*—it is with the affections in Love, as with the Reason in Religion—we cannot *diffuse* & equalize—we must have a SUPREME—a *One the highest.*"[117] At first blush, this might seem to suggest that the prime analogate is married love, but the context—as well as all Coleridge's other work—makes it clear that married love is the highest only on the *human* level. What gives even this its ultimate meaning is love of God, for just a few lines earlier in the same passage Coleridge had already affirmed that "a happy marriage" is itself "the symbol of the Union of the Church with Christ; that is, of the Souls of all good Men with God, the Soul of the Universe."[118] And of course "symbol" for Coleridge is the means of communicating the deepest kind of reality.[119]

Thus the prime analogate for all love is love of God. As Coleridge wrote toward the end of his life, "The Crown and Base, the Pinnacle and Foundation of a regenerate and truly Christian State of Mind . . . is to love God in all that we love, to love that only therefore in which we can at the same time love God—and thus gradually, in the growth toward our final perfection, more and more to love all things in God." The goodness and meaning of all created things—and thus their capacity for being loved—have their origin, and indeed their continued existence, from God: "In rever-

---

116. Notebook 21 ½, f. 50 (1819–1820). One of Coleridge's Shakespeare lectures of 1811–1812 offers a more explicit reference to such a Platonic "ladder of love": "One infallible criterion in forming an opinion of a man is the reverence in which he holds women. Plato has said, that in this way we rise from sensuality to affection, from affection to love, and from love to the pure intellectual delight by which we become worthy to conceive that infinite in ourselves, without which it is impossible for man to believe in a God. In a word, the grandest and most delightful of all promises has been expressed to us by this practical state—our marriage with the Redeemer of mankind" (*SC,* 2:107).

117. *CM,* 1:752.

118. *CM,* 1:751.

119. On Coleridge's idea of symbol, see my book *The Symbolic Imagination: Coleridge and the Romantic Tradition,* esp. chap. 1.

encing the good and wise man I reverence the Father of Lights, even the Tri-une God, who is *essentially* the Good, the True and the Wise: and of whom all other Goodness, Truth & Wisdom is but a participation, an infusion." One should not be too surprised to hear an echo of Neoplatonic philosophy here, for this remarkable notebook entry concludes: "By the bye, there are passages worthy almost of an inspired Christian in the Aeneads [*sic*] of Plotinus on the subject of Love in all its' genuine forms as so many exercises of the Love of the Supreme Being."[120] In all that we love, it is "the surpassing Loveliness of the Infinitely Good, that we love, and desire."[121]

Coleridge's life, as we know, did not realize all these ideals of love. His broken marriage, his unfulfilled love for Sara Hutchinson, his estrangement from several of his brothers, his ruptured relationship with Wordsworth, the strains his opium addiction put on so many of his friendships—all point to a failure to live out the lofty ideals he believed in. Yet for all that, Coleridge lived much of his life surrounded by love, both given and received. This complex story will be unfolded in the following chapter, but for the moment this much can be said: Coleridge's ideals of love were lofty indeed and, whatever his own failures, he never lost faith in the validity of those ideals.

120. Notebook 47, ff. 3, 5 (1 October 1830).
121. Notebook F, f. 66v (26 June 1827).

I languish after Home for hours together, in vacancy; my feelings almost wholly unqualified by Thoughts. . . . After I have recovered from this strange state, & reflected upon it, I have thought of a man who should lose his companion in a desart of sand where his weary Halloos drop down in the air without an Echo.—I am deeply convinced that if I were to remain a few years among objects for whom I had no affection, I should wholly lose the powers of Intellect—Love is the vital air of my Genius.

—*Letter to Mrs. S. T. Coleridge, 12 March 1799*

CHAPTER 2

Love in Coleridge's Life

Coleridge's ideal of love was lofty indeed. However, in T. S. Eliot's words, "Between the idea / And the reality . . . / Falls the Shadow," and the reality of Coleridge's life was certainly deeply shadowed. There are worlds of self-knowledge in such a cry as this sad and all too typical passage from one of his notebooks: "I am loving & kind-hearted & cannot do wrong with impunity, but o! I am very, very weak—from my infancy have been so."[1] Coleridge would have been the first to agree with Southey's assessment of him: "he labours under a disease of the volition."[2]

Coleridge believed, of course, in the innate weakness of will of all human beings, since the finite will is from its birth not in conformity with the "Absolute Will." He wrote in his "Confessio Fidei" of 1810: "I believe, and hold it as the fundamental article of Christianity, that I am a fallen creature; that I am of myself capable of moral evil, but not of myself capable of moral good, and that an evil ground existed in my will, previously to any given act, or assignable moment of time, in my consciousness."[3] However, it was also evident that other human beings laboring under the same weakness overcame it, while he did not. He had only to compare himself with such pillars of probity as Wordsworth and Southey to realize his own inadequacy. To Southey, he confessed to "the knowledge that I am of no significance, relatively to, comparatively with, other men, my contemporaries," going on in the same letter to speak of "a sense of weakness—a haunting sense, that I was an herbaceous Plant, as large as a large Tree, with a Trunk of the same Girth, & Branches as large & shadowing—but with *pith within* the Trunk, not heart of Wood / . . . This on my honor is as fair a statement of my habitual Haunting, as I could give before the Tribunal of Heaven."[4]

The same sort of self-knowledge is revealed, although by indirection, in a comment about his son Hartley twenty years later: "He has neither the resentment, the ambition, nor the Self-love of a man. . . . With this is connected his want of a salient point, a self-acting principle of Volition—and from this, again, arise his shrinking from, *his shurking* [*sic*], whatever requires and demands the exertion of this inward power, his

---

1. *CN*, 2:2091 (May 1804).

2. *New Letters of Robert Southey*, ed. Kenneth Curry, 2:118 (17 March 1815).

3. *LR*, p. 16. On Coleridge's view of the relation of will to the Christian doctrine of original sin, see my *Coleridge and Christian Doctrine*, pp. 114–19.

4. *CL*, 2:959 (1 August 1803).

cowardice as to mental pain, and the procrastination consequent on these."[5] Surely the father recognized all too clearly the legacy he had given to this gifted and beloved son; Coleridge's disease, like Hartley's, was "his want of a salient point, a self-acting principle of Volition." Coleridge may have been playing here, too, with the etymology of *salient:* Hartley (like himself) lacked a "jumping-off place," a strong center that would allow him to act freely and responsibly—to go out of himself with the confidence that there was something to come back to. I suggest that the "salient point" lacking in himself was something he also found missing in Hartley: self-love, a sense of his own worth. As Coleridge admitted, he saw in himself good intentions but weakness of will—soft pith instead of a "heart of Wood." A consideration of Coleridge's childhood will give us some clue as to the source of this sense of inadequacy.

Frankly, it is difficult to trust Coleridge's own recollections of his childhood. Although we must of course take account of Coleridge's remembrances, his tendency to self-dramatization makes some of them suspect. It is difficult to take literally, for example, his remark to Sir George Beaumont that "I was hardly used from infancy to Boyhood; & from Boyhood to Youth most, MOST cruelly."[6] The context may offer at least a partial explanation of this jaundiced view: about to leave for Malta, he was explaining to Sir George the background of the illnesses for which he hoped Malta would be a cure. Certainly Coleridge's parents did not treat him "hardly," much less "cruelly." As he admitted in a more sanguine mood, "My father was very fond of me, and I was my mother's darling."[7] This was clearly his more usual view, that he was loved by his parents and that he returned their love. However, he did add to this claim of his parents' special fondness for him the significant phrase: "in consequence I was very miserable." Being the youngest of ten children, and being more than a little spoiled and favored by his parents—and at the same time being intellectually precocious—young Samuel was bound to arouse a certain resentment among his elder siblings. But, except for the famous incident of his brother Frank (next above him in age) tormenting him over a piece of cheese—resulting in Samuel's running away and his traumatic overnight exposure to the elements—there is little evidence that he was as a child treated harshly by his family. He was of course, even early on—and by his own admission—a young eccentric, with his dreaminess and his bookish ways, but among his family there seems to have been as much pride in his early intellectual accomplishments as there was resentment. Even Frank, the brother with whom he had the most strained relationship, seems to have alternated (no doubt bewilderingly for young Samuel) between contempt and affectionate admiration. If there was a tyrant at all during his boyhood, it may have been his nurse, Molly, who seems to have resented Samuel being preferred over her favorite, Frank.

Whatever may be said of Coleridge's parents (to whom we shall return shortly), his relations with his brothers (his only sister Ann having died, we recall, while he was still at Christ's Hospital) were spotty at best. This may be in great part because he was sent away to school at Christ's Hospital in London at the age of ten, remaining there until

5. *CL,* 5:232 (Late May 1822).
6. *CL,* 2:1053 (1 February 1804).
7. Quoted by E. K. Chambers, *Samuel Taylor Coleridge: A Biographical Study,* p. 5.

he entered Cambridge at nineteen. Later, even after he left Cambridge, his literary plans and ambitions kept him away from his native Devonshire. The result of all this was not necessarily that his brothers did not care about him, or he about them, but may have been very simply that they did not know each other very well.[8] A notable exception was George Coleridge, eight years the poet's senior, who came to London in 1785 as a schoolmaster, and who began to play a father's role for the lonely boy. Although Coleridge's relationship with George became strained in later years, it was unquestionably one of the more supportive relationships of his boyhood years.

* * *

Clearly, all these fairly ordinary and essentially external circumstances do not go far to explain Coleridge's deep-seated feelings of personal inadequacy—his unworthiness to be loved—such feelings as are expressed in this notebook entry of 1805: "I wish to love even more than to be beloved & am so haunted by the conscience of my many Failings that I find an unmixed pleasure in esteeming & admiring, but in Esteem & Admiration I feel as a man whose good dispositions are still alive feels in the enjoyment of a *darling* Property on a doubtful Title. My instincts are so far dog-like."[9] The result of such feelings was, of course, that it was difficult for him to believe that he was loved: "I have never had anyone, in whose Heart and House I could be an Inmate, who loved me enough to take pride & joy in the efforts of my power, being at the same time so by me beloved as to have an influence over my mind."[10]

What then, if not "hard usage and cruelty" suffered in boyhood, was the source of Coleridge's pervasive sense of inadequacy? Thomas McFarland, writing of Coleridge's multiple and complex problems—his weakness of will, his hypochondria, his addictive personality, his deceits and plagiarisms—conjectures that "a massive *anxiety*, rather than any more specific ailment, was the true source of Coleridge's varied miseries." Furthermore, he continues, "if we seek the origin of an anxiety so pervasive, so shattering and so neurotically persistent as Coleridge's, we look, in this post-Freudian age, almost as a matter of course to his childhood. Even before more precise investigation, one might suspect that his position as the youngest of ten children, nine of whom were brothers, was psychologically precarious. The likelihood of fragmentation of attention and relation on the part of the parents, and of damaging aggressiveness from the jealously competing brothers, would inevitably be high in such a situation." I would single out in particular what McFarland calls a "primal anxiety, arising from his relationship with his mother."[11]

Obviously, to track this Freudian "anxiety" we must look beyond what Coleridge

---

8. Coleridge's brother James, in 1814, wrote dismissively that he thought his brother quite mad: "What a humbling lesson to all men is Samuel Coleridge" (quoted by Chambers, *Samuel Taylor Coleridge,* p. 267); it was only in 1818, when Coleridge was forty-six and James fifty-nine, that they seem to have discovered the value of each other's friendship (ibid., p. 313).

9. *CN,* 2:2726 (November–December 1805).

10. *CL,* 3:307 (12 March 1811, to Henry Crabb Robinson).

11. *Romanticism and the Forms of Ruin: Wordsworth, Coleridge, and Modalities of Fragmentation,* pp. 113–14.

knew consciously and was willing to admit, either to himself or to anyone else. One might consider first the importance he attached to mother love, as in a passage we have cited earlier: "There is a religion in all deep love, but the Love of a Mother is . . . the veil of softer Light between the Heart and the heavenly Father!"[12] Yet how curious it is that, for all the burden of significance Coleridge gave to a mother's love, he said so little about his own mother. He spoke of his father with evident affection, but of his mother only with respect. In the second of his famous five autobiographical letters written in 1797 to Thomas Poole, Coleridge wrote at some length and with affectionate good humor of his learned and good-hearted father; of his mother he said simply that she was "an admirable Economist, and managed exclusively."[13] Not a word more before going on to speak of his brothers and their accomplishments. His mother is mentioned again in two of the later autobiographical letters: once when he records the incident of the "crumbly cheese" and young Samuel's traumatic night by the riverside, noting that his mother was "almost distracted" when he did not return home by nightfall and "outrageous with joy" upon his safe return; and again when he tells of her delight in his recounting of the grammatical gaffes of his teacher Parson Warren.[14] Coleridge's father is mentioned again and again in these letters, always glowingly, but of his mother there is nothing beyond these momentary glimpses.

Even more telling is the fact that his mother's death in 1809 is nowhere recorded in Coleridge's writings, even though there is a warm and detailed account of the death of his father.[15] There are circumstances equally strange in the time leading up to her death. Notified that his mother was near the end, Coleridge professed himself unable to make the trip from Grasmere to Ottery St. Mary. In the course of a letter to Southey that relates some bits of public gossip and some business details concerning the pub- lication of *The Friend,* Coleridge announces that he has heard from his brother George that "my poor Mother is near her end, and dying in great torture . . . & she wishes to see me before her death—But tho' my Brother knows I am penniless, not an offer of a Bank note to en[able] me to set off. In truth, I know not what to do—for [there] is not a shilling in our whole House."[16] The letter immediately continues with chitchat about Byron, Godwin, and others, with no further mention of his mother's impending death. Even granting that the journey from the Lakes to Somerset is a long one, and that his circumstances were no doubt straitened, it is still curious that Coleridge should have passed off onto his brother the blame for his inaction. This is not to imply that he did not love his mother, but simply that his feelings for her may have been at least unconsciously ambiguous.

From here it is only a short step to the suspicion that he may not have been in fact, as he claimed, his mother's favorite, but that her attitude toward him was much more mixed. McFarland offers a very cogent analysis: any claim that Coleridge was any

12. *CL,* 5:180 (20 October 1821). Something of this same anxiety about his relationship with his mother may be latent in his letter to his son Derwent, then aged seven, about the sacredness of a mother's love; see Chapter 1, n. 50.

13. *CL,* 1:310.

14. *CL,* 1:353–54, 387–88.

15. *CL,* 1:355 (16 October 1797).

16. *CL,* 3:261 (Early November 1809).

more than occasionally his mother's favorite "must surely be either fantasy or what psychoanalysts call a 'screen memory,' for had he in any deep sense been his mother's darling, his self-confidence, as in our post-Freudian sophistications we all now know, would have been far greater than it was. If we judge by the results, his mother's affection must have alternated with periods of neglect or coldness, which developed an extreme anxiety in the child. According to psychoanalytic theory, moreover, it developed rage and an equally great guilt in response to the rage."[17]

Against this background, one might conjecture that Coleridge's being sent away to London for school only a year after his beloved father's death would have seemed a rejection by his remaining parent—an "exile" that was to remain in effect for nine years, to be followed by still another departure, this time to Cambridge.[18] Thus his experience of "home" only included the first nine years of his life, and even that was an experience of ambiguity. With this in mind, one is less surprised to find the following revealing comment in a letter to Thomas Poole on the occasion of the death of Poole's mother in 1801: "I have learnt, Poole! that your Mother is with the Blessed.—I have given her the tears & the pang, which belong to her Departure; & now she will remain to me for ever what she has long been, a dear & venerable Image, often gazed at by me in imagination, and always with affection & filial piety. She was the only Being whom I ever *felt* in the relation of Mother."[19] Coleridge's emphasis on *felt* is all too eloquent.

Are we to conclude that Mrs. Coleridge was an unnatural mother who deliberately withheld love from her youngest child? No, by all accounts she seems simply to have been a woman with emotional limitations of her own: perhaps overmethodical, excessively ambitious for her children, relatively undemonstrative in comparison with her husband. As Dr. James Gillman wrote of her (with Coleridge as his source, we may assume), "She was, I should add, a very good woman, though like Martha, over careful in many things, very ambitious for the advancement of her sons in life, but wanting perhaps that flow of heart which her husband possessed so largely."[20] McFarland concludes: "No great crime, surely, but her diminished store of warmth, further dissipated by the natural demands of caring for nine other children, could have seemed to

17. *Romanticism and the Forms of Ruin,* p. 116. McFarland's whole treatment of Coleridge's relationship with his mother is excellent and very illuminating; see pp. 113–18. The psychoanalyst David Beres was the first to show how Coleridge's relationship with his mother must have been marked by a singular coldness. See "A Dream, A Vision, and a Poem: A Psycho-Analytic Study of the Origins of *The Rime of the Ancient Mariner,*" esp. pp. 101–4.

18. Dr. James Gillman records an observation of Coleridge's that suggests that Coleridge himself, at least retrospectively, was conscious of some such feeling: "When I was first plucked up and transplanted from my birth place and family, at the death of my dear father, whose revered image has ever survived in my mind, to make me know what the emotions and affections of a son are, and how ill a father's place is likely to be supplied by any other relation, Providence (it has often occurred to me) gave the first intimation, that it was my lot, and that it was best for me, to make or find my way of life a detached individual, a Terrae Filius, who was to ask love or service of no one on any more specific relation than that of being a man, and as such to take my chance for the free charities of humanity" (*The Life of Samuel Taylor Coleridge,* pp. 11–12, note).

19. *CL,* 2:758.

20. *Life of Samuel Taylor Coleridge,* pp. 6–7. For the biblical allusion to the story of the sisters Martha and Mary, see Luke 10:38–42.

her infant son to be total abandonment, and the anxiety thus generated would be very great indeed."[21]

Whatever Coleridge's unconscious feelings and motivations may have been, his conscious awareness of the limitations of familial relationships in his life is made clear in a letter to his nephew John Taylor Coleridge late in his life: "All the circumstances of my life and all the good and all the faulty ingredients of my character, have unhappily joined in nipping or diverting the growth of the affections of consanguinity."[22] Among these "faulty ingredients" of Coleridge's character must be included his chronic inability to face tension or unpleasantness, probably because, in his anxiety, he feared rejection. It may be reasonably conjectured that it was this unwillingness or inability to face unpleasantness that made Coleridge lie to his brothers about his bad debts, his academic failures, and his general dissolute behavior at Cambridge—and drove him to his short-lived enlistment in the Dragoons; that prompted him to stay away from his brothers for years on end, fearful of their fully justified reproaches at his professional and domestic failures; and that even kept him from his mother's deathbed. As Molly Lefebure says, Coleridge "feared, above all, the intrusion of harsh realities within the context of the affections," for he was "not suited, either by temperament or experience, to deal with the realities of this earth, neither in the guise of money matters and what Poole called 'the common concerns of life,' nor in the shape of the emotional vicissitudes which are an integral part of day-to-day living, and especially part of family circumstance."[23]

All too often, too, Coleridge's evasions of family responsibility brought on feelings of guilt, which he then, not infrequently, shrugged off onto his brothers: it was *they* who neglected *him,* they who failed to appreciate his gifts. Some of this guilt was brought on, in fact, by his brothers' kindnesses to him, especially during his Cambridge years. Knowing that they had made considerable personal sacrifices for him, and realizing that he had largely wasted his gifts at the university, he was cast into a morass of guilt from which he could escape only by blaming them for their imagined unkindness and neglect.

But for all his failures in familial relationships, Coleridge never lost his belief in the importance of family affections. In the same letter to his nephew John Taylor in which he confessed that the "faulty ingredients" of his character had "nipped or diverted the growth of the affections of consanguinity," he went on to insist not only that such affections were important to him but also that in his later years he was able to recover some of his family ties: "It has certainly additionally endeared you and your Sister Fanny to me, that with regard to both I first felt in the full force that those affections had been only suppressed & driven to the root, not killed or alienated." In fact these "affections of consanguinity" did flower in Coleridge's later years—in what E. K. Chambers calls the "Indian summer" of the years 1824–1830 at Highgate[24]—in his warm and affectionate relationships with various of his nephews and nieces, notably with William Hart Coleridge, son of his brother Luke, and three sons of his brother

21. *Romanticism and the Forms of Ruin,* p. 117.
22. *CL,* 5:356 (19 April 1824).
23. *The Bondage of Love: A Life of Mrs. Samuel Taylor Coleridge,* p. 77.
24. See *Samuel Taylor Coleridge,* p. 313.

James—the barrister John Taylor, the Eton schoolmaster Edward, and especially Henry Nelson, who was to marry Coleridge's daughter Sara and become the devoted posthumous editor of several of his uncle's works. In this same period, too, the earlier strained relationships with his brothers James and George were healed, and there was in Coleridge a general sense of affectionate peace with his family.

*　*　*

If Coleridge held up "married friendship" as the ideal of conjugal love, the reality of his married life was, sad to say, quite otherwise. Whom to blame? Coleridge himself never settled that notorious debate, nor are we likely to do so here. In any case, there is plenty of blame to go around among the three parties to the event: Coleridge, Sarah, and Robert Southey.

Certainly it began badly. Sometime during his year and a half at Cambridge, Coleridge had begun to experience the deepening of his feelings toward Mary Evans, whose family had been wonderfully kind to him during his last four or five years at Christ's Hospital; they had been, in fact, a kind of surrogate family for him. Now, after his departure from the university and in the throes of the ill-fated Pantisocracy scheme with Southey, Coleridge found himself torn between the kind of conventional family life that seemed to be held out by Mary Evans and his commitment to the new community on the banks of the Susquehanna. In the midst of plans for the Pantisocracy, Coleridge had become engaged to Sarah Fricker, sister of Southey's fiancée Edith. What could be more convenient and pantisocratic? Meanwhile, however, Mary Evans heard news of the Pantisocracy project and wrote to call it absurd and extravagant, hardly even believing he could seriously consider it.[25] Realizing how deep his feelings were for Mary, Coleridge's faith began to waver. Southey, however, was unbending: Coleridge must hold to the true faith. Discovering then that Mary Evans was herself engaged to be married, Coleridge wrote frantically to Southey, clearly casting about for a release from his obligation to Sarah Fricker. "I am calm, dear Southey! as an Autumnal Day, when the Sky is covered with grey moveless Clouds. . . . To lose [Mary Evans]!—I can rise above that selfish Pang. But to marry another—O Southey! bear with my weakness. Love makes all things pure and heavenly like itself:—but to marry a woman whom I do *not* love . . . !" But then he concluded distressingly: "Mark you, Southey!—*I will do my duty.*"[26] Surely here was a cry for release; but Southey was resolute, coming to London, tracking Coleridge down where he was lingering in a fit of anxious indecision, and bringing him back to Bristol—to Pantisocracy and Miss Fricker.[27]

25. Ibid., p. 33.

26. *CL*, 1:145 (29 December 1794).

27. It is remarkable that there are still critics who excuse Southey for his role in Coleridge's marriage to Sarah Fricker. Even so judicious a biographer as Jack Simmons (perhaps out of his affection for Southey) affirms, "It is too much to expect that Southey, at his age and with all his own preoccupations at the time . . . should have realised the full significance of Coleridge's . . . references [in a letter to Southey on 21 October 1794] to 'her whom I do not love, but whom by every tie of reason and honour I ought to love'" (*Southey*, pp. 56–57). Perhaps, Simmons suggests, Coleridge's protestation was "less

This was hardly an auspicious beginning for a marriage, but Coleridge would try to put the best face on it. As W. J. Bate astutely remarks, Coleridge "could never live for long in an atmosphere not completely friendly. When confronted with feelings of hostility or annoyance, his first impulse was to approach them directly, half admit their reasonableness, and seek to palliate them with resolves of reform and with open and generous admiration of the other person."[28] Such was his reaction to Southey in this instance. Southey had done him incalculable harm in insisting on his marriage, but Coleridge was his usual forgiving, self-deprecating self. He wrote to a friend at this time that Southey's "Genius and acquirements are uncommonly great—yet they bear no proportion to his moral Excellence—He is truly a man of *perpendicular Virtue*."[29] With Sarah, too, he would make the best of it. Perhaps he could make love happen by sheer dedication and force of will. And perhaps it *did* happen, for he wrote to Thomas Poole a few days after his wedding that he was "united to the woman, whom I love best of all created Beings."[30]

Coleridge and Sarah seemed happy enough for a time, briefly at Clevedon and then in their more famous cottage at Nether Stowey—Coleridge domesticating in house and garden, writing poetry and political tracts, occasionally preaching in neighboring churches—and they both seemed to take unbounded joy in the arrival of their son Hartley. But within several years cracks began to show, just as the weeds began to take over Coleridge's garden. In his *Conciones ad Populum* of 1795, Coleridge had spoken of the importance of the "domestic affections" in building up society—a sentiment very consonant with the ideals of the Pantisocracy. What he soon discovered, however, was that the good of society was not enough; fulfillment of the individual was also important, and it was here that his marriage evidently began to be found wanting. It was not, I think, as has often been suggested, that Sarah Fricker was not sufficiently intelligent; all the evidence suggests that she was intelligent above the ordinary. It was not simply that she was not interested in intellectual and artistic endeavors, though it is true that she was of a more practical turn of mind than Coleridge. Nor was the problem what Coleridge later portrayed as her quick temper. She was, in fact, an intelligent, attractive, and quite admirable woman, who has been maligned by many of us in our desire to defend Coleridge.

---

plain to Southey than it would have been to most men, for even at this early age he had an unusually high sense of duty" (p. 49). As Coleridge wrote to Southey during the period of his vacillation over the engagement, "Your undeviating Simplicity of Rectitude has made you too rapid in decision—having never erred, you feel more *indignation* at Error, than *Pity* for it" (*CL*, 1:106). Had Southey only felt more pity than indignation for Coleridge in this difficult situation, perhaps a tragic marriage might have been averted.

A more recent biographer of Southey, Ernest Bernhardt-Kabisch, takes a sterner view than Simmons concerning Southey's role: "Southey, too obtuse, inflexible, or both to see anything more than lack of resoluteness in his friend's palpitations, merely lectured him and, finally, went to look for him in London and persuaded him to return to Bristol and to Sarah. We should not make Southey wholly responsible for the older man's marital mistake. But we must regret his officiousness and impercipience" (*Robert Southey*, pp. 24–25).

28. *Coleridge*, p. 20.

29. *CL*, 1:152 (Late February 1795).

30. *CL*, 1:160 (7 October 1795). Does the phrase "first of all created Beings" also suggest that Coleridge sublimated his feelings by intellectualizing them?

The real reason for the separation of Coleridge and Sarah seems to me best discovered in the perceptive comments about Sarah made by her daughter many years later, which suggest that her mother and father were simply temperamentally too different to live peaceably under the same roof:

> The sort of wife to have lived harmoniously with my father need not have possessed high intellect or a perfect temper—but greater enthusiasm of temperament than my mother possessed. She never admires anything she doesn't understand. Some women, like . . . Mrs. Wordsworth, see the skirts of a golden cloud—they have unmeasured faith in a sun of glory and a sublime region stretching out far beyond their ken, and proud and happy to think that it belongs to them are ready to give all they have to give in return. This faith, this docility, is quite alien to the Fricker temperament . . . They are too literal . . . And then my mother's very honesty stood in the way—unless at the same time she had possessed that meekness and forbearance which softens everything and can be conciliating by utter silence on all unpeaceful topics and the constant recurrence to soothing cheering themes. . . . she has no taste whatever for abstractions and formerly had less toleration for what she did not relish than now.[31]

In light of this description, it is perhaps no wonder that, as Molly Lefebure very shrewdly points out, "only one man held her unadulterated admiration and that was Robert Southey."[32] The steady and resolute Southey was her model of what a man— even a literary man—should be as a husband: not a man who dwells with mystery and uncertainty but a man of clear mind and steady principles, not a man who backs away from confrontation but a forthright man who speaks his mind and acts on his principles. Sarah could never have abided the irresolute Coleridge for a lifetime, any more than he could have abided the clearheaded Sarah. Very simply, there were between them—in the classic phrase of the divorce courts—"irreconcilable differences."

Another factor, of course, was the perpetual shadow of Coleridge's inability to deal with emotional discomfort or unpleasantness. Sarah's often reasonable complaints about the practicalities of the household and domestic economy or about child-rearing—or, more importantly, her protestations about her husband's increasing use of opium—were too often perceived by Coleridge as a rejection of himself or as a willful failure to understand the needs of a man of genius. His response to such protestations by Sarah was all too often to escape over Dunmail Raise to the sympathetic ears of the Wordsworths, or to the idealized love of Sara Hutchinson, or to patient friends like Thomas Poole who were always ready to soothe him. The ultimate result, of course, was pain for all concerned: for his wife because of his slighting of her, for his friends because of the burden of misery he laid on them, and for himself because of the guilt he inevitably came at last to feel. As Southey once wrote, "Never I believe did any other man for the sake of sparing immediate pain to himself inflict so much upon all who were connected with him, and lay up so heavy and unendurable burthen of self condemnation."[33]

---

31. Earl Leslie Griggs, *Coleridge Fille: A Biography of Sara Coleridge*, pp. 104–5; quoted by Molly Lefebure, "'Toujours Gai': Mrs. Samuel Taylor Coleridge, 'A Most Extraordinary Character', Reviewed in the Light of Her Letters," p. 118.

32. "'Toujours Gai,'" p. 114.

33. *New Letters of Robert Southey*, ed. Curry, 2:3–4.

The separation of the Coleridges was, in fact if not in formal decision, more or less complete by the time of Coleridge's return from Malta in 1806. By this time his illness and his growing dependence on drugs had exacerbated his native indisposition to face difficult situations, and the thought of dealing with the differences between Sarah and himself was intolerable to him. Divorce was for him—for religious reasons but no doubt also, unconsciously, for psychological reasons—out of the question, so a separation was arranged. Initially, Coleridge was to take care of the boys, Hartley and Derwent, while his wife was to take care of the daughter, Sara; but, before long, and no doubt inevitably, more and more responsibility passed into Mrs. Coleridge's hands. For all the years to come—though Coleridge later roused himself to concern for the university education of the boys—it was she who accepted primary responsibility for the care of the children. On the whole over the years he was moderately faithful in assuming (if not always fulfilling) financial responsibility for his wife and children, even at times in quite practical ways, such as an insurance policy on his life. However, it was only in later years, beginning about 1820—by which time Coleridge had been securely established with the Gillman family for four years—that Coleridge was able to establish genuine personal relationships with his children. These soon became, at least on his part, warm and loving, as Coleridge by turns agonized over Hartley's problems at Oxford, fretted over Derwent's career plans, and watched romance blossom between Sara and his respected young nephew Henry Nelson Coleridge.

To the end of his life Coleridge was (often with the help of friends, especially Southey) to remain faithful—in his fashion—to his responsibilities for his family. In the course of time Mrs. Coleridge came to see the separation as a sensible decision and to accept this strange marital arrangement. In 1822, Mrs. Coleridge could come to Highgate with Sara for a peaceful monthlong visit; Coleridge, for his part, could write to his friend Dr. Green in 1832—on the occasion of Mr. and Mrs. S. T. Coleridge's joint appearance at the baptism of their grandchild Edith—"bating living in the same house with her there are few women, that I have a greater respect & *ratherish* liking for, than Mrs. C."[34] Not the ideal marriage, to be sure, but not the worst of relationships, either.

*   *   *

As we turn to consideration of romantic love in Coleridge's life, I would like to begin by conjecturing that Coleridge was "in love" (a term he himself used) three times in his life. The first time was with Mary Evans, his love for whom grew slowly and naturally out of the kindness of the Evans family—that loving circle of widowed mother, amiable son, and two charming daughters—which became his surrogate family during his lonely years at Christ's Hospital. As Coleridge and Mary matured, they were drawn together by an attraction not only of body and emotions but also of spirit. As Coleridge wrote to Southey about Mary Evans, only weeks before his engagement to Sarah Fricker, "Her Image is in the sanctuary of my Heart, and never can it be

34. *CL,* 6:918 (6 August 1832).

torn away but with the strings that grapple it to Life."[35] Even in the midst of his reluctant engagement to Sarah he wrote to Southey about Mary Evans: "She was VERY lovely, Southey! We formed each other's minds—our ideas were blended."[36] I conjecture further that it was precisely the hasty and ill-advised engagement to Sarah, occasioned by his equally ill-advised enthusiasm for Pantisocracy, that made him realize the depth of his love for Mary. But by then it was too late, and she was engaged to another man.

Then, I believe he *did* fall in love with Sarah Fricker, because he needed desperately to be in love after his loss of Mary. We do not always fall in love wisely, nor on this occasion did Coleridge. Like many another, before and after, he allowed his own needs and the evident attractions of the other to outweigh prudential considerations. Many of us fall in love, however, without marrying the object of our affections. Coleridge's mistake was not in falling in love, but in marrying against his own instinctive better judgment. If romantic love does not grow and deepen into what Coleridge would call friendship, which involves the union of minds he had found with Mary Evans, it can only wither and die, as in this case it rather quickly did.

Coleridge's relationship with Sara Hutchinson—which was of course to be the great love of his life—began, as did his relationship with Mary Evans, in a natural setting. The setting was once again a loving family, or rather two—the Hutchinsons and the Wordsworths—with both of whom (unlike the Frickers) Coleridge felt very much at home. This time—in contrast to his relationship with Mary Evans—it seems to have been the romantic attachment that came first, for within weeks of first meeting the Hutchinsons he was secretly holding Sara's hand by the fireside. From that moment, he wrote, "love struck me with its light—and alas poisoned and incurable—dart."[37] In this case, however, the emotional attachment clearly deepened into friendship, without ceasing to be romantic. As with Mary Evans, there was a genuine community of interests: poetry, reading, the whole world of ideas—things for which Sarah Fricker had little patience. Sara Hutchinson could laugh with him, share his ideas, help him with the transcription of his writing, and encourage him by her understanding presence.

The friendship deepened as the years went on; so even more did Coleridge's passion for Sara, making their situation even more difficult for them both. As early as 1801, two years after the beginning of their relationship, Coleridge wrote in one of his notebooks: "A lively picture of a man, disappointed in marriage, & endeavoring to make a compensation to himself by virtuous & tender & brotherly friendship with an amiable Woman—the obstacles—the jealousies—the impossibility of it."[38] The relationship clearly remained "virtuous"; there is no evidence of any sexual consummation ever occurring. But it was considerably more than brotherly, as the depth of Cole-

---

35. *CL*, 1:88 (13 July 1794). The lines are repeated in a letter to Henry Martin a few days later; see *CL*, 1:92 (22 July 1794).

36. *CL*, 1:123 (3 November 1794).

37. *CN*, 1:1575 (October 1803, written in remembrance of 24 November 1799). The letter has the quoted phrases in Latin: "amor me levi spiculo, venenato, eheu! et insanabili, &c"; the translation is my own.

38. *CN*, 1:1065 (December 1801).

ridge's passion during these years attests. A notebook passage from 1806 is representative: "I know, you love me!—My reason knows it, my heart feels it / yet still let your eyes, your hands tell me / still say, o often & often say, My beloved! I love you / indeed I love you / for why should not my ears, and all my outward Being share in the Joy—the fuller my inner Being is of the sense, the more my outward organs yearn & crave for it / O bring my whole nature into balance and harmony."[39]

However, for all the depth of feeling evident here, there was also a process of idealization in Coleridge's relationship with Sara Hutchinson. She was not only the actual Sara who soothed him and acted as his amanuensis, she was also the idealized "Asra," whom it was safe to love because she made no demands on him. Having no familial responsibilities toward her, Coleridge could indulge his flights of fancy that it was she—not Sarah of the demanding domestic hearth—who was his true ideal "other." This process was no doubt assisted by Coleridge's continuing use of opium, which eased his escape from the demands of the reality he could not face.

What kind of woman was the *real* Sara Hutchinson? She was far from a beauty, by all accounts, except for her long, lovely, fine brown hair—which Coleridge's daughter, perhaps a bit unkindly, called "her only beauty."[40] But her other personal attractions were evidently many: intelligence, wit, a great sense of fun, an affectionate nature, a clearheaded honesty about herself and others. Although we have little left to document her feelings for Coleridge, it seems clear that while she returned Coleridge's love, she did not do so in the same emotional measure. This may have been a function of her clear-minded honesty: a fulfilling future with Coleridge, for all her love and admiration for him, was out of the question. George Whalley says of her that she was "strong, sane, independent; she had a sense of humour which was also a fine sense of proportion; she had a vein of 'shrewdness.'"[41] She was clearly able, better than Coleridge, to accept the ultimate impossibility of their situation. Thus, when the break between Coleridge and Wordsworth came in 1810, it was clear to Sara where her future must lie. George Whalley notes: "Despite her ten years' attachment to Coleridge, she was not to be drawn from the large and demanding circle of life which the Wordsworth and Hutchinson families had come to represent to her. Coleridge, the comet—fiery, portentous—spun on into the darkness, hungering for love and understanding, inveterately gregarious, incurably alone."[42] It was the end of Coleridge's intimacy not only with the Wordsworths but also with Sara.

* * *

For all that, I cannot agree with Whalley that Coleridge was "incurably alone." He

---

39. *CN,* 2:2938 (November–December 1806). This may be why, by the time of his departure for Malta in 1804, Coleridge was feeling even more deeply the hopelessness of his situation. It has even been suggested that one reason for the Malta sojourn was to try to wean himself away from Sara; see *CN,* 2:2860n. If this is the case, clearly the attempt was unsuccessful.

40. See George Whalley, *Coleridge and Sara Hutchinson,* p. 143.

41. Ibid., p. 149.

42. Ibid., pp. 149–50.

might have been a failure in marriage and in romantic love, but he was not a failure in friendship. Coleridge had, in fact, an extraordinary gift for friendship. The kinds and degrees of closeness were of course, as in the lives of any of us, of a considerable range. Something of this range in Coleridge's life is suggested by a charming letter to his dear friend Dr. James Gillman, originally written (probably in 1825) in the flyleaves of a copy of *Aids to Reflection*. It begins with five lines of verse, entitled "The Three Kinds of Friends":

Tho' Friendships differ endless *in degree*,
The *Sorts,* methinks, may be reduced to Three:
*Ac*quaintance many; and *Con*quaintance few;
But for *In*quaintance I know only two,
The Friend, I've mourn'd with, and the Maid, I woo!

My dear Gillman,
    The ground and 'materiel' of this division of one's friends into *Ac*- Con- and *In*-quaintance was given by Hartley Coleridge, when he was scarcely five years old. On some one asking him, if Anny Sealy (a little girl, he went to school with) was an Acquaintance of his, he replied very fervently, pressing his right hand on his heart—No! She is an *In*quaintance. 'Well! 'tis a Father's tale!'—& the recollection soothes your old

Friend & *In*quaintance
S. T. Coleridge[43]

Gillman was of course one of the sturdiest and best of Coleridge's friends, but he was only one of what sometimes seems a multitude. Charles Lamb naturally has a place of special honor, not only for longevity but also because of the depth of his and Coleridge's mutual love. They were "blue-coat boys" together at Christ's Hospital beginning in 1782 (when Coleridge was only ten); although Lamb was three years younger, the two boys formed a friendship that was to last until death, which came to both of them, perhaps fittingly, in the same year. Lamb's sister Mary, for whom Coleridge also had a great affection, was almost as much a part of this long and intimate friendship as was her brother. Another old and valued friend from Christ's Hospital days was the poet George Dyer, who was a regular attendant at Coleridge's Thursday evening soirees at Highgate forty years later. There is a remarkable loyalty in the kind of friendship that can survive the ups and downs of life from boyhood to old age.
    Southey was also of course an early and important friend of Coleridge, though their intimacy was destined not to continue. In their early years, the two young idealists shared their dreams, but in time the differences between them became too many: Coleridge bridled for a time at Southey's abandonment of Pantisocracy in favor of the law; and Southey later became deeply disillusioned at Coleridge's lack of responsibility. Like the dutiful soul he was, Southey assumed much of the responsibility for Coleridge's family, but he was never able finally to forgive Coleridge for his weakness. It says much about the two men that Coleridge, in his will, spoke specifically of Southey as one for whom he had special esteem; while Southey wrote, upon hearing of Cole-

43. *CL,* 5:466 (May 1825?).

ridge's death, "He had long been dead to me"—and continued, quite unjustly: "All who were of his blood were in the highest degree proud of his reputation, but this was their only feeling concerning him."[44] Perhaps a touch of Coleridgean weakness in himself might have made Southey more understanding, and hence more forgiving.

And what of Wordsworth? Here perhaps the rift went even deeper, precisely because the bond had been so strong, the relationship—the "symbiosis," as Thomas McFarland calls it—so important to both of them. The rupture of a year and a half— brought about by the meddling of a mutual friend but occasioned and no doubt exacerbated by Coleridge's opium dependency—though patched up through the good offices of Lamb and Henry Crabb Robinson, left scars that never disappeared. The forgiveness between Coleridge and Wordsworth was no doubt genuine, and much of the deep esteem and love were still there, but the old intimacy could never return.

It was not long after the reconciliation of Coleridge and Wordsworth, on the occasion of the deaths of Wordsworth's children Catherine and Thomas, that Dorothy Wordsworth wrote a most revealing comment about Coleridge. Coleridge had written feelingly to Wordsworth about the death of Thomas in December 1812, and both Dorothy and their mutual friend Catherine Clarkson tried to persuade Coleridge to visit Grasmere, as a means of comforting William. Coleridge, however, seems not to have been able to face the pain of returning to Grasmere under such changed circumstances. Dorothy finally wrote to Catherine Clarkson:

> He will not let himself be served by others. Oh, that the day may come when he will serve himself! Then will his eyes be opened, and he will see clearly that we have loved him always, do still [love] him, and have ever loved—not measuring his deserts. . . . God bless him. He little knows with what tenderness we have lately thought of him, nor how entirely we are softened to all sense of injury. We have had no thoughts of him but such as ought to have made him lean upon us with confidential love, and fear not to confess his weaknesses.[45]

What Dorothy is sketching out here, with her customary astuteness, is Coleridge's need to be able to accept "unconditional love," his need to believe that he could be loved not for his intellectual gifts or his charm or his goodness, but for himself, as he was, with all his weaknesses—"not measuring his deserts." He had to realize that he could not, and need not, *earn* the love of his friends—whether by his work or by his virtue or even by his love—but that it was a gift freely given. Perhaps his failure to do so at this time has to do with his sense of himself: he could not expect others to forgive him his weaknesses, because he had not yet forgiven himself.

But the time was to come, in later years, when he did achieve the kind of insight Dorothy wished for him. Such a change may date, I suggest, from the beginning of his domestication with the Gillmans in Highgate, when, perhaps for the first time since early childhood, he felt he had a real home, where he felt accepted as he was and not as someone might wish him to be. There is a remarkable passage in the *Biographia Liter-*

44. Quoted by Chambers, *Samuel Taylor Coleridge,* p. 330.
45. *The Letters of William and Dorothy Wordsworth,* ed. E. de Selincourt, 2d ed., vol. 3, *The Middle Years,* rev. by Mary Moorman and Alan G. Hill, pt. 2, pp. 556–57 (6 April 1813).

aria, in the letters on Charles Maturin's *Bertram* that Coleridge used to pad out his second volume. Coleridge is writing about the Spanish *Don Juan,* and finds himself intrigued by its view of love:

> To be capable of inspiring in a charming and even a virtuous woman, a love so deep, and so entirely personal to *me*! that even my worst vices, (if I *were* vicious!) even my cruelty and perfidy, (if I *were* cruel and perfidious) could not eradicate the passion! To be so loved for my *own self,* that even with a distinct knowledge of my character, she yet died to save me! . . . it is among the [mysteries], and abides in the dark ground-work of our nature, to crave an outward confirmation of that *something* within us, which is our *very self,* that something, not *made up* of our qualities and relations, but itself the supporter and substantial basis of all these. Love *me,* and not my qualities, may be a vicious and an insane wish, but it is not a wish wholly without a meaning.[46]

It is significant that this passage first appeared in the *Courier* in September 1816, just months after the beginning of Coleridge's residence with the Gillmans, where at last he had found a home—where love without conditions became at least a possibility for him.

It is perhaps for some such reason that one begins to see, during the Highgate years, a flowering of new, rich friendships in Coleridge's life. Some of the old friends—like Lamb and Dyer, the splendid and loyal Thomas Poole, Basil and Mrs. Montague, the J. J. Morgans, Sir George and Lady Beaumont—remained for the most part faithful and close; but a host of new ones began to appear at Highgate as Coleridge, now more content with—or more resigned to—who he was, could open himself more honestly and more comfortably to others. Preeminent, of course, were the Gillmans themselves: those gracious, generous-hearted people, who gave Coleridge a kind of unquestioning love he had perhaps never felt before, because only now was he ready for it. Then there was Joseph Henry Green: doctor, disciple, but above all devoted friend, from 1817 to the very end, when he sat by Coleridge's deathbed. Thomas Allsop was a young man to whom Coleridge wrote, over a period of more than ten years, some of his most moving letters on friendship; they seem to have drifted apart during the last five years of Coleridge's life, but for many years the relationship was a close and cherished one. The Swedenborgian C. A. Tulk was a devoted friend to Coleridge all during the Highgate years, as was the Jewish scholar Hyman Hurwitz. It was also during these years that the learned John Hookham Frere, mentioned in Coleridge's will as one of his most esteemed friends, entered his circle, never to leave it; so too the noted Dante scholar H. F. Cary. Coleridge's publisher Daniel Stuart was more than a business associate; he was a caring and dedicated friend. The German merchant Charles Aders and his wife, Eliza, were intimate friends of Coleridge for over twenty years. And in the last years came a whole new generation of loving friends, the young people who became his devoted disciples, and whose devotion he returned, like his nephew Henry Nelson Coleridge, James Gillman, Jr., John Sterling, and the young Highgate native Adam Steinmetz.

All this is not to say that Coleridge was the perfect friend, that he never failed in the offices of friendship, but that he was a good and loving friend to many, who in turn loved him. The Highgate years, whatever their hardships and failures, were golden years of friendship for Coleridge.

* * *

Deeply bound up with Coleridge's acceptance, later in his life, of himself as he was, was his growing acceptance of God's unconditioned love of him. There was One who knew him, with all his weaknesses and failures, and yet loved him. He was redeemed from his weakness by a loving Savior and cherished by a loving Father.

Coleridge's sense of the *possibility* of redemption from his sinfulness very likely began about the time of his first articulation of his return to Trinitarian Christianity, in Malta in 1805, after several years of flirtation with Unitarianism. This conversion was intellectual on one level, to be sure, but on another, deeper level, it was a response to his sense of his own unworthiness, and hence of his need for a redeemer. Just days after his first recorded expression of his belief in the Trinity, he issued this anguished cry: "Have Mercy on me, O something *out* of me! For there is no *power* . . . in aught *within* me! Mercy! Mercy!"[47] Coleridge's belief in the Trinity was always very much bound up with his belief in the doctrine of Redemption. However, although he came fairly early to believe in Redemption by Christ, it was many years before he came to feel that redemptive forgiveness as a fact in his own life. He was able to come to it only as he came to realize that forgiveness, the mercy he prayed for, was synonymous with love. As he expressed this truth much later, in 1832, "the love of an almighty I AM to a fallen & suffering Spirit becomes Mercy. To Spirits Conformed to the Holy Will the I AM is the God of *Love*—to a fallen Spirit the God of *Mercy*. Love and Mercy are the same attribute differenced only by the difference in the Objects." This attribute, whether manifested as Mercy or as Love, is based on God's "perpetual presence to each, his living, life-giving Presence."[48]

Between these two moments, more than twenty-five years apart, there was little substantive change in Coleridge's belief about the Christian doctrine of Redemption, but there was enormous growth in Coleridge himself. Again, I suggest that his growing acceptance of God's forgiving love in his own life was bound up, at least in some measure, with his move toward a greater acceptance of himself, which in turn had roots in the willingness of others to forgive him—the Gillmans, Lamb, his host of Highgate friends. It would be futile, I believe, to try to assign priority or causality: did his forgiveness of himself precede his ability to accept forgiveness from others or from God? Or was it his acceptance of God's forgiveness that allowed him to forgive himself? The theologian in me (and here I think Coleridge would be similarly tempted) is prompted to give the priority to God, pouring out His love and eliciting love in others. But perhaps one should be content to call it a kind of "mutual causality," by which love, wherever it begins, prompts a rebound of love, initiating an unending circle or

---

47. *CN*, 2:2453 (15 February 1805).
48. Notebook F, f. 85v (6 March 1832).

(to use a favorite Coleridgean image) an "eddying" of love, drawing into itself God and self and others.

The deeply personal prayer that became more and more part of Coleridge's life during the years at Highgate was increasingly humble and yet increasingly confident: humble in his realization of his own inadequacy, confident in God's forgiving and strengthening love. For prayer is, he wrote in a personal notebook late in his life, "the mediation—or rather the effort to connect the misery of Self with the blessedness of God."[49] Again: "awakening in myself the firm faith in his Presence I offer to him his own best gifts, the yearnings of my spirit after him, the Father of Spirits."[50] Coleridge was a loving and much-loved man, even to the end, when his dear friends Green and Gillman sat by his deathbed. But it was in God that Coleridge found at last the only perfect response to the "yearnings of his spirit."

49. Notebook F, f. 75 (7 January 1830).
50. Notebook 42, f. 38 (November 1829).

Methinks, it should have been impossible
Not to love all things in a world so fill'd.

— *"The Eolian Harp"*

CHAPTER 3

The Conversation Poems:

"Love and Joyance"

People are always finding new paradigms for Coleridge's conversation poems. I was set on the trail of mine by a paragraph of John Beer in his splendid edition of Coleridge's *Poems*. At the beginning of his section headed "Friendship with Wordsworth," Beer sees Coleridge, in the summer of 1797 and again early in 1798, turning away from current politics to the world of nature, proclaiming his aim in poetry as being "to elevate the imagination & set the affections in right tune by the beauty of the inanimate impregnated, as with a living soul, by the presence of Life."[1] In doing so, Coleridge believed himself to be turning away from "immediate causes"—political forces and influences—to causes less immediate but more lasting, to be found in the world of nature.

Turning from Beer's familiar quotation to the letter to George Coleridge from which it was taken, I discovered—what I had not noticed before—that the passage is followed very shortly after by a quotation from Wordsworth, eighteen lines of which originally formed part of the conclusion to *The Ruined Cottage:*

> Not useless do I deem
> These shadowy Sympathies with things that hold
> An inarticulate Language: for the Man
> Once taught to love such objects, as excite
> No morbid passions, no disquietude,
> No vengeance & no hatred, needs must feel
> The Joy of that pure principle of Love
> So deeply, that, unsatisfied with aught
> Less pure & exquisite, he cannot chuse
> But seek for objects of a kindred Love
> In fellow-natures, & a kindred Joy.
> Accordingly, he by degrees perceives
> His feelings of aversion softened down,

---

1. Samuel Taylor Coleridge, *Poems,* ed. John Beer, p. 115. The quotation is from a letter of Coleridge to his brother George, 10 March 1798; *CL,* 1:397.

A holy tenderness pervade his frame!
His sanity of reason not impair'd,
Say rather that his thoughts now flowing clear
From a clear fountain flowing, he looks round—
He seeks for Good & finds the Good he seeks.[2]

Here, it seemed to me, was a lovely expression of what Coleridge had been doing, for the past two or three years, in his conversation poems. Perhaps Wordsworth's expression of the experience could shed some light on Coleridge's own expression of it in his poems.

What we find in the Wordsworth quotation is essentially a passage from one kind of love—or level of love—to another, through the mediation of nature. If nature is "inarticulate" as an object of love, it is also blessedly innocent: it excites "no morbid passions . . . no vengeance & no hatred." Unlike mankind, nature can put one in immediate touch with the "pure principle of Love." Having once tasted that "pure principle," as if having drunk at a pure fountain, one searches for the same taste in one's "fellow-natures." Delightedly, the searcher finds there the goodness that is sought; what had been thought of as corrupt and impure, is now found to contain a goodness hitherto unseen. One's vision has been changed, one's eyes have been opened:

. . . his thoughts now flowing clear
From a clear fountain flowing, he looks round—
He seeks for Good & finds the Good he seeks.

Turning to Coleridge's conversation poems, I find essentially the same pattern repeated in the six that are most commonly called by that name: "The Eolian Harp" (August 1795), "Reflections on Having Left a Place of Retirement" (1795), "This Lime-Tree Bower My Prison" (June 1797), "Frost at Midnight" (February 1798), "Fears in Solitude" (April 1798), and "The Nightingale" (April 1798). It is significant that all these poems, in which Coleridge finds the "pure principle of Love" not only in nature but also in his "fellow-natures," were written during some of the happiest years of his life. The first, "The Eolian Harp," is of course intimately associated with the honeymoon period of his marriage to Sarah Fricker, and their relationship—for all its ups and downs—remained relatively serene and hopeful during these three years, as Hartley and Berkeley were born and their world remained full of possibilities. Add to this that during this time Coleridge was writing steadily and even found employment with the *Morning Post,* and that his friendship with Wordsworth was in its golden time, and it becomes clear why the very personal "conversation poems" of this period seem so effortless and full of joy.

Although it may have been written slightly later in 1795 than "The Eolian Harp," I begin with "Reflections on Having Left a Place of Retirement" because it offers a clearer and more complete example of the pattern I am proposing. In "The Eolian Harp," as I shall suggest, the pattern, though begun, is broken before its completion.

2. *CL,* 1:397–98.

Like all the conversation poems, "Reflections" early establishes the presence of a beloved other or others. Although the setting of these poems is invariably a landscape, the natural surroundings are primarily a vehicle for human presence. As M. H. Abrams points out, "Romantic writers, though nature poets, were humanists above all, for they dealt with the non-human only insofar as it is the occasion for the activity which defines man: thought, the process of intellection."[3] I would add that if it is thought that "defines" man, for Coleridge it is finally only love that can fulfill him. Hence the presence of the beloved is crucial in these "Poems of Friendship," as George McLean Harper so aptly termed them.[4]

But if love is crucial to the experience of Coleridge's conversation poems, so too is joy, for love and joy are deeply and closely interrelated. As Wordsworth wrote in the passage from *The Ruined Cottage* with which we began, the one who has learned to love nature "needs must feel / The Joy of that pure principle of Love." We saw in our analysis of Coleridge's ideal of love that, in Coleridgean terms, love by its nature has three essential characteristics: it is instinctive, it is essentially one, and it is complementary to one's self; we saw too that love is by nature not constrictive but expansive. All these characteristics are crucial here. We saw that the act of love, as instinctive, is not primarily a movement of the mind, rationally decided upon, but of the heart, which—when it has achieved a "habit of love"—moves naturally and spontaneously toward what is perceived as good. In this movement, the heart can only move toward something or someone with whom it has a kinship, for love is analogous with all other love, as being is analogous with all other being. But finite being, precisely as finite, constantly reaches out to other being as complementary of itself, while it itself is at the same time complementary of others. Finite being, in effect, expands itself in the act of love.

If love is primarily a *power*—the power by which we reach out, in an "expansion of being"—to other being kindred with our own, joy is the *effect* of this movement of power. It is, quite literally, the experience of ecstasy—the experience of "standing outside" ourselves—that the power of love allows us to achieve. However, this ecstatic joy, this exaltation of the heart outside itself, is not a movement into an abyss of abstract delight. It is an ecstasy of communion with "the other," in which the giving and receiving of love is bonded into a celebration of shared being and goodness. Joy can never be truly a solitary experience, for it is precisely the exultation that comes from a sense of loving communion with another human being, with nature, or with God.

The deepest joy of all, as Wordsworth implies—and as we shall see in Coleridge's conversation poems—is the joy that comes from communion with the "pure principle of Love." This is, of course, what we saw in our analysis of Coleridge's "ideal of love" to be the prime analogate, in which the perfection of love is found in its fullness: "our nature imperiously asks a *summit*, a *resting-place*—it is with the affections in Love, as

3. "Structure and Style in the Greater Romantic Lyric," in *Romanticism and Consciousness: Essays in Criticism*, ed. Harold Bloom, p. 202.

4. "Coleridge's Conversation Poems," in *English Romantic Poets: Modern Essays in Criticism*, ed. M. H. Abrams, 2d ed., p. 189.

with the Reason in Religion . . . we must have a SUPREME—a One the Highest."[5] But the prime analogate (Coleridge's *natura naturans*) is not merely a "resting-place" but an active source of being and life. As the "supreme," it contains the fullness of the power attributed to it and is therefore necessarily the source of that power in those beings that share it in a finite degree. It is, quite literally, a "principle"—or, as the ancient philosophers called it, a "principium"—"id ex quo aliquid fluit": "that from which something flows." The implicit metaphor of the fountain falls nicely to the point here, for it is a favorite of Coleridge, connoting activity, continuity, and life-giving energy. For Coleridge, the "pure principle of Love" can only be the active, ever-flowing, and life-giving energy of God, the prime analogate of all being, all goodness, and all love.

In the interaction of love and joy there is, too, an ongoing sense of process, as the conversation poems will make clear, for love and joy are so intimately related that they nourish and strengthen each other. Love of nature leads to joyous communion with it, communion leads to new and deeper perception, which leads in turn to new love and its consequent joy.

It may be helpful at this juncture to recall Coleridge's search for a "home." It was only where he felt himself loved that he could experience the joy that would allow him fully to exercise his creative gifts, for the support of the loved and loving "other" was crucial to the working of Coleridge's imagination. Such a longing for a home may explain what he most admired about the sonnets of William Lisle Bowles, who is acknowledged to be Coleridge's master in the meditative lyric.[6] Bowles's sonnets, Coleridge says, "domesticate with the heart, and become, as it were, a part of our identity."[7] Coleridge's conversation poems, too, it might be said, "domesticate with the heart." They are in a sense, whatever their specific setting, poems of the hearth-side, which assume—or create—a domestic "space" in which the poet and his beloved, spouse or child or friend, can exist together in joyful harmony. Meena Alexander, analyzing the "phenomenology" of the conversation poems, speaks of "a personal space which is upheld in the tension between the meditating consciousness and the human other. The presence of the other is of vital importance to the meditation. Only within a space where the other is potentially available can the self be maintained."[8]

* * *

However, the dimensions of love at the beginning of each poem differ significantly from poem to poem. "Reflections on Having Left a Place of Retirement" opens with a blissful but very limited view of love. The young couple are together, to be sure, sharing the stillness and seclusion of a sheltered spot of beauty: the rose, the thick jasmines, the "green and woody" landscape, the sea's "faint murmur" in the distance (ll. 1–7). They are, however, clearly sequestered from the larger world; the emphasis is

5. *CM*, 1:752
6. See Abrams, "Structure and Style in the Greater Romantic Lyric," pp. 212–17.
7. *PW*, 2:1139.
8. *The Poetic Self: Towards a Phenomenology of Romanticism*, p. 37.

on their isolation, as the poet contemplates, somewhat patronizingly, Bristowa's "wealthy son of Commerce" sauntering by (l. 11). They are happily—and virtuously—domesticated there; the man of Commerce, on the other hand, has only come to the country for a Sabbath walk to calm for a moment his "thirst of idle gold" (l. 13).

But although this is a "Valley of Seclusion" (l. 9), it is also a place surrounded and filled by nature, which draws the poet out of his preoccupation with his spouse and himself in their isolation, to a moment "when the Soul seeks to hear; when all is hush'd, / And the Heart listens!" (ll. 25–26). The sense of blessedness ("we *were* bless'd," l. 18) and joy ("the inobtrusive song of Happiness," l. 23) that the poet feels in the intimate landscape shared with his beloved leads his soul more deeply into the felt experience of nature, to the grander perception of nature from the top of the mountain. As Coleridge later makes clear in "Dejection," it is joy that is

> the spirit and the power
> Which wedding Nature to us gives in dower
> A new Earth and new Heaven.
> (ll. 67–69)

Just as clearly joy is the outcome of his loving encounter here with "Omnipresence."

> No *wish* profan'd my overwhelméd heart.
> Blest hour! It was a luxury,—to be!
> (ll. 41–42)

Joy is thus the power that links the poet with nature, as well as earthly reality with reality beyond, and at the same time it is the power that celebrates their union; joy is both a cause of love and the inevitable result of loving encounter.

Thus through hearing with his heart the inarticulate language of nature (an "inobtrusive song," an "unearthly minstrelsy," ll. 23–24), the poet is brought to a new vision—an awareness of, in the words of Wordsworth's lines from *The Ruined Cottage*, the "pure principle of Love." As in Coleridge's philosophizing about love, so in his poetry: love is ultimately one, and one kind or level of love can lead to another; love is sustained and nourished by other love. Here, through the mediation of joy, the poet's love for his spouse has opened him to the love of nature, and in nature he finds love in its purity: in (as Wordsworth said) "such objects, as excite / No morbid passions, no disquietude." (Even the commercial gentleman from Bristol could sigh, and say it was a blessed place.) In nature the poet discovers a broader scope for his love, because he has achieved a sense—indeed "a sense sublime"—of a larger presence than either his own or even the shared presence of the loving couple:

> It seem'd like Omnipresence! God, methought,
> Had built him there a Temple: the whole World
> Seem'd *imag'd* in its vast circumference.
> (ll. 38–40)

His vision enlarged, his heart opened by this experience of a transcendent reality,

I

the poet now returns to the "quiet Dell" (l. 43) with a more generous view of love and with a new sense both of purpose and of obligation toward others.9 He can no longer "dream away the entrusted hours / On rose-leaf beds" (ll. 46–47) but must go forth to share in active love the gifts he has been given. The "Valley of Seclusion" will always remain a sacred spot for him, to which he will often come in spirit, but now his heart has opened so that he can wish the peace of such a place not only for himself but for all. In the sweeping movement of this poem—from domestic love and love of a particularized natural scene (the "little landscape" of line 6), to visionary insight into the "power" of nature itself, returning then to home and the intimate landscape with a broadened view of the meaning of love—we may find fulfilled what Morris Dickstein calls Coleridge's "deepest impulse," to "reconcile the visionary imagination with ordinary human bonds, with family and domesticity, with love, with social benevolence."10

This is, in essence, the pattern I find repeated, with appropriate variations, in the other conversation poems: the poet begins with a view of love that is in some way significantly limited; he is touched by nature, whether its serenity or its power or simply its beauty; through this touch of nature, the poet moves—or is moved—into a higher realm, where, in a visionary experience, he feels "the Joy of that pure principle of Love"; finally he returns to the ordinary world with a new, more generously loving view of those around him. The "return," of course, and the broadening of view are commonplaces in criticism of the conversation poems. What has not been sufficiently noted, however, is the intermediate stage: the momentary movement into a higher kind of world—transcendent or numinous—where one can experience love in its purity, taste pure love (in Wordsworth's phrase) "from a clear fountain flowing." In Coleridgean terms, this stage is a passage from the *natura naturata* to the *natura naturans,* from an experience of the effect—the bird, the flower, the landscape, the natural fact—to an experience of the process itself.11 The poet can love fully only when he has

9. In using the term *transcendent reality,* I should explain that by this (here and elsewhere) I do not mean necessarily a "mystical" encounter—that is, a direct and immediate apprehension of God—but the transcendent made immanent in created nature. Implicit here, as I believe is generally true in Coleridge, is a sacramental view of nature: nature, including human nature, as a vehicle for the revelation of the divine. See my book *The Symbolic Imagination: Coleridge and the Romantic Tradition,* chap. 1.

10. "Coleridge, Wordsworth, and the 'Conversation Poems,'" p. 374. George Watson, too—though without showing its relationship to Coleridge's visionary experience—singles out the "ordinariness" of the concerns and attitudes of the conversation poems: "the deep, broad, domestic affections of father, husband and friend that the poetry of Europe has elsewhere tended to neglect as too modest, fleeting, and undramatic a theme" (*Coleridge the Poet,* p. 62).

11. Although my argument does not depend on them, it may be helpful to justify my use of Coleridge's terms *natura naturata* and *natura naturans.* Coleridge's simplest definition is found in a note in his manuscript *Logic,* where he refers to *natura naturata* as "nature as the aggregate of objects" and *natura naturans* as "nature considered as an agent" (*Logic,* ed. J. R. de J. Jackson, in *The Collected Works of Samuel Taylor Coleridge,* ed. Coburn, p. 45). In one of his lectures on the history of philosophy, Coleridge says: "The aggregate of phenomena ponderable and imponderable, is called nature in the passive sense,—in the language of the old schools, *natura* NATURATA—WHILE THE SUM OR AGGREGATE OF THE POWERS INFERRED AS THE SUfficient causes of THE former (which by Aristotle and his followers were called the SUBSTANTIAL FORMS) is nature in the active sense, or *natura natur*ANS" (*Philosophical Lectures,* ed. Kathleen Coburn, p. 370; this passage is taken from Coleridge's lecture notes, and the

bathed in the fountain, the source, the "principle of Love." Like the classic spiritual travelers, he must pass through a stage of purification, which is also (as for them) a means of enlarging his vision. In order fully to love, in other words, he must experience the "prime analogate" of love that gives meaning and importance to all the other loves of his life.

* * *

"The Eolian Harp" begins, once again, with a very limited view of love, circumscribed by the comforts of domesticity. "Most soothing sweet it is" (l. 2)—a perfect phrase to express the safe and comfortable kind of love the poet is feeling. At first the elements of nature serve only to reinforce his experience: the "white-flower'd Jasmin, and the broad-leav'd Myrtle, / (Meet emblems they of Innocence and Love!)"; the slow-moving clouds; the "star of eve / Serenely brilliant"; the homely scent of the bean field; the murmur of the sea heard only in the distance (ll. 3–12). It is very much the intimate "little landscape" of "Reflections on Having Left a Place of Retirement."

But the image of the lute (l. 12), the wind harp, introduces a motif of freedom. Although the Eolian harp is first intimated as a metaphor for the poet's spouse—"by the desultory breeze caress'd, / Like some coy maid half yielding to her lover" (ll. 14–15)—as its strings are "boldlier swept" (l. 18) the harp begins to evoke a larger "spirit," a wider-ranging breath of life that moves through nature—and even beyond. The wind cannot be restrained, but of its very nature moves outward, touching whatever is in its path, carrying with it melodies that are "Footless and wild, like birds of Paradise, / . . . hovering on untam'd wing!" (ll. 24–25). In the later version, of course, this not wholly satisfying expression of the "pure principle of Love" is deepened into:

> . . . the one Life within us and abroad,
> Which meets all motion and becomes its soul.
> (ll. 26–27)[12]

Under the press of such an experience, the poet is moved far beyond mere domesticity into a sense of the need for universal Love:

---

curious forms of emphasis are his own).

My point in using the term *natura naturans* is that the poet is in touch in the conversation poems not only with nature as "effect" but also with its "causes"; not only with nature as an object but also with the very process of nature, which includes a glimpse even of its deepest source and cause. Since Coleridge calls the *natura naturans* "nature considered as an agent," we might even go on to say that the poet is in touch not only with nature as an object but with nature as "subject," whom it is possible to "encounter." As Coleridge says in his essay "On Poesy or Art," the *natura naturans* "presupposes a bond between nature in the higher sense and the soul of man. . . . man's mind is the very focus of all the rays of intellect which are scattered throughout the images of nature" (in *Biographia Literaria*, ed. J. Shawcross, 2:257–58). As Coleridge had affirmed two or three pages earlier in the same essay, "nature itself is to a religious observer the art of God" (p. 254).

12. Lines 26–33 were first published in Coleridge's *Sibylline Leaves* in 1816.

> Methinks, it should have been impossible
> Not to love all things in a world so fill'd.
>
> (ll. 30–31)

Once again, joy is a mediating power. Early in the poem, the spirit of joy is in a low key ("most soothing sweet it is," l. 2), but it becomes more intense as the wind rises ("over delicious surges," l. 19), coming to fullness in the poet's perception of the "one Life" ("joyance every where," l. 29), in which the poet clearly feels a kind of ecstatic union of love with "all things."

The passage that follows, in the aftermath of his ecstatic joy, shows the poet reclining tranquilly on "the midway slope / Of yonder hill" (ll. 34–35), as passive as the "subject Lute" (l. 43). The reflection that there teases his "indolent and passive brain" (l. 41) is reminiscent (though the poet here is purportedly less active than Wordsworth) of one of Wordsworth's reflections following a "spot of time" in *The Prelude,* in which the poet tries to fathom the meaning of his experience. Here the poet reflects that what he has experienced is indeed a divine reality: "one intellectual breeze, / At once the Soul of each, and God of all" (ll. 47–48).

But this is mere speculation—"shapings of the unregenerate mind" (l.55); the real experience was the affective encounter with the "one Life" a few moments before, an encounter of the heart. Perhaps this is part of the reason for his feelings of guilt: he is indulging these "idle flitting phantasies" (l. 40) when he should be opening his heart to the powers of nature; he is *thinking,* instead of responding to the call to *love* "all things in a world so fill'd." Rather than a fear of pantheism, as has often been asserted, what his wife's "more serious eye" (l. 49) alerts him to may be the idleness of philosophical speculation itself: he should be loving and praying in faith rather than idly philosophizing.

At the same time, the poet's feelings of guilt may also be due, at least in part, to something much more mundane (unexpressed but none the less effective), his wife's desire not to allow the circle of the poet's love to become too large, the desire, on the part of a wife who is perhaps jealous of his preoccupation with a world she cannot share, to return him to the safe and comfortable circle of domesticity. Whatever the reason, the effect is to cut short, abruptly, the outward movement of the poet's spirit and return him to where he had begun: "Peace, and this Cot, and thee, heart-honour'd Maid!" (l. 64). With the other conversation poems, it is axiomatic that in the "return" at the end one is aware of a change in the poet, an enlarging of his view of himself and of the world. Here, uniquely, one feels not enlargement but restriction, an acceptance of limitation, a narrowing of focus. It is a pattern begun but not completed—or, perhaps more accurately, a pattern abruptly broken.

This is by no means to say that the poem is a failure. The very breach of the pattern that has been begun creates, in effect, a new pattern: an unresolved conflict, a tension between two polarities of Coleridge's life at this time—the life of the mind ("these shapings of the unregenerate mind") and the life of the heart ("Faith that inly *feels,*" l. 60). It is a tension that Coleridge was never wholly to resolve, and his expression of it here is both magisterial and deeply moving.

* * *

In "This Lime-Tree Bower My Prison" the pattern is, happily, unbroken. The limitations of the poet's attitude are evident in the opening lines: the lime-tree bower is a prison. The poet is concerned, not with his friends, but with himself; it is *his* lost beauties and feelings he mourns. His melodramatic—not to say slightly ludicrous—reflection about his friends, "whom I never more may meet again" (l. 6), betrays the strong undernote of self-pity. His lime-tree prison is actually the prison of the self.

But as his imagination begins to work with the scene, as in his mind the poet follows the progress of his friends across the well-known landscape, the power of nature begins to assert itself: the "springy heath," the "hill-top edge," "that still roaring dell," where the "branchless ash" trembles and a "dark green file of long lank weeds / . . . nod and drip beneath the dripping edge / Of the blue clay-stone" (ll. 7–20). Set free from his own self-pity by looking outside himself, he can now follow his friends with greater sympathy and openness; as he imagines them emerging into a broader view— "beneath the wide wide Heaven" (l. 21)—his own thoughts can range even more widely and grandly. His thoughts now are no longer bounded by the lime-tree bower or even the imagined dell but move across "the many-steepled tract magnificent / Of hilly fields and meadows" (ll. 22–23) to the sea, the sunset, the richly burning clouds— and again the sea. Through this gradually unfolding and broadening panorama of natural landscape he is brought to a moment of visionary experience, a glimpse of a reality beyond the material, as he sees himself stand

> Silent with swimming sense; yea, gazing round
> On the wide landscape, gaze till all doth seem
> Less gross than bodily; and of such hues
> As veil the Almighty Spirit, when yet he makes
> Spirits perceive his presence.
>
> (ll. 39–43)

Once again the poet has touched, as it were, the very source of life, "the pure principle of Love." Here is in fact, only lightly veiled, the "Almighty Spirit" itself, and the experience is of spirit perceiving Spirit.

The joy that acts as catalyst for his experience is this time, I suggest, what the poet imagines as the joy of his absent friends, who "wander in gladness" along "the hill-top edge" (ll. 7–8) and down into the shaded dell, and again—after they have emerged from the wooded dell into the light of "the wide wide Heaven"—still "wander on / In gladness all" (ll. 26–27). They rejoice (as he does in imagination) in the beauty continually unfolding before them. But "most glad" of all is "gentle-hearted Charles," who stands (the poet imagines) "struck with deep joy" (l. 38) at the beauty of the landscape spread out before him; and it is the joy-struck Charles with whom the poet most identifies himself, remembering how he too was moved by the same deep joy:

> So my friend
> Struck with deep joy may stand, as I have stood,
> Silent with swimming sense; yea, gazing round
> On the wide landscape . . .

> . . . of such hues
> As veil the Almighty Spirit, when yet he makes
> Spirits perceive his presence.
>
> (ll. 37–43)

Love and joy are intermingled here: the poet's love of nature, of Charles, of the Almighty; Charles's joy in the imagined scene, the poet's own joy in the remembered scene, and the poet's rejoicing in the joy of his beloved friend.

It is no wonder, then, that the poet's response is a deepening of his joy:

> A delight
> Comes sudden on my heart, and I am glad
> As I myself were there!
>
> (ll. 43–45)

No wonder either that, as the poet returns to himself, the lime-tree bower is no longer a prison but a spot of nature quite as sacred as the grander scene he has just witnessed in imagination. The same "Spirit" is everywhere, within us and abroad:

> Henceforth I shall know
> That Nature ne'er deserts the wise and pure;
> No plot so narrow, be but Nature there,
> No waste so vacant, but may well employ
> Each faculty of sense, and keep the heart
> Awake to Love and Beauty!
>
> (ll. 59–64)

Thanks to the bonds of love—between man and nature, between the poet and his friend—and the Spirit of love that pervades all, the poet finds that there is a joy, paradoxically, even in the deprivation of joy:

> sometimes
> 'Tis well to be bereft of promis'd good,
> That we may lift the soul, and contemplate
> With lively joy the joys we cannot share.
>
> (ll. 64–67)

How natural then that this newly awakened and broadened sense of love, which allowed the poet to escape from self-pity, should reach out at the close in a blessing of love for the "gentle-hearted Charles" (l. 68). Having experienced love in its purity in his joyful moment of vision, the poet's own heart has been freed from self-love and self-seeking.

* * *

In "Frost at Midnight," the limitation of love is not betrayed by anything so blatant as self-pity. It is revealed, rather, in the image the poet settles on as a metaphor for himself in the quiet opening scene by the fireside on that frosty night—the fluttering film on the grate:

> Methinks, its motion in this hush of nature
> Gives it dim sympathies with me who live,
> Making it a companionable form,
> Whose puny flaps and freaks the idling Spirit
> By its own moods interprets, every where
> Echo or mirror seeking of itself,
> And makes a toy of Thought.
>
> (ll. 17–23)

The poet, the "idling Spirit," is thinking not of others—he only glances at the child sleeping by his side—but of himself.

Once again it is something from nature, here a bit of unconsumed ash from a fire, that begins the outward movement, in this case a movement in time rather than space, a movement of memory. Here, however, nature is initially nothing quite so grand in its working as it was in "This Lime-Tree Bower"; it is less cause than occasion, a reminder of childhood days. It is crucial nonetheless, especially since its likeness to the poet, as "the sole unquiet thing" (l. 16), is set off by the silence of all the other natural things around the cottage: sea, and hill, and wood. As always, nature is an indispensable part of the process.

Joy too is, as always, an agent in the process, but here—in this beautifully muted poem—its presence is less obvious. In fact, the word *joy,* uniquely in these poems, does not appear at all. The presence of joy itself, however, is unmistakable. Its seeds may be discerned in the poet's opening meditation, in which he experiences a sense of union with the film that flutters on the grate, giving it "dim sympathies with me who live." Taking its cue from the fluttering wisp of ash, the poet's "idling Spirit" recalls a long-ago sight of that same film, which as a child he had watched flutter in the fire while he dreamt of his "sweet birth-place" (l. 28). This in turn prompts him to hear again the bells of childhood, which

> rang
> From morn to evening, all the hot Fair-day,
> So sweetly, that they stirred and haunted me
> With a wild pleasure, falling on mine ear
> Most like articulate sounds of things to come!
>
> (ll. 29–33)

Thus the movement of the poem is in the direction of a deeper intensity of feeling: from "dim sympathies" to sweetness to the stirring and haunting of "wild pleasure." It should come as no surprise, then, when the poet's childhood remembrance climaxes with "my heart leaped up" (l. 40) at the half-opening door of the classroom.

This deepening of feeling, from sympathy into joyful anticipation, sets the mood for the refocusing of his gaze from past to present, to his sleeping child cradled next to him. His remembered joy from childhood sparks newly felt joy in the presence of his child:

> My babe so beautiful! it thrills my heart
> With tender gladness, thus to look at thee.
>   (ll. 48–49)

Thus feeling comes in aid of feeling, joy in aid of love, and the beautiful benediction that closes the poem is a blessing not only of love but also of joyful hope.

But what is perhaps most striking here about the poet's use of the pattern we have been considering is the merging of two stages: the poet's awareness of the higher realm of experience—his sense of the *natura naturans*—and his return to the world of everyday reality with a more generous heart. Here it is precisely in the blessing of his child that he is able to articulate his vision of the transcendent:

> But *thou,* my babe! shalt wander like a breeze
> By lakes and sandy shores, beneath the crags
> Of ancient mountain, and beneath the clouds,
> Which image in their bulk both lakes and shores
> And mountain crags: so shalt thou see and hear
> The lovely shapes and sounds intelligible
> Of that eternal language, which thy God
> Utters, who from eternity doth teach
> Himself in all, and all things in himself.
>   (ll. 54–62)

The poet's memory of his own childhood has finally turned his attention away from himself to the sleeping child by his side, who till now had been only another element in the quiet setting around him. His heart now opened, he can express in the form of a blessing his awareness of a higher realm of being and experience, which can give substance and meaning to his whole encounter with nature and human life. The "therefore" of the closing paragraph—"Therefore all seasons shall be sweet to thee" (l. 65)—flows directly from his awareness of the role of the transcendent in his consciousness of the world. Once again, the experience of nature—the mediation of the *natura naturata* and his fresh awareness of the *natura naturans*—has brought the poet to a broader sense of the meaning and obligations of love. And, one might add, the thought that was only a "toy" in his idle reverie by the fireside has become an instrument of serious meditation and profound insight.

* * *

"Fears in Solitude," by far the longest of the conversation poems, is also unique in that it has no single clear addressee; for the most part it is addressed, by turns, to God and to England. As in the other conversation poems (except for "The Nightingale," as we shall see), the poet begins with a significantly limited view of his relationship to the world around him. Here the limitation is, if we may identify the poet with the "humble man" (l. 14) who lies in the "small and silent dell" (l. 2), that his view of nature has something of the quality of dream, and hence of unreality:

> . . . his senses gradually wrapt
> In a half sleep, he dreams of better worlds,
> And dreaming hears thee still, O singing lark,
> That singest like an angel in the clouds!
> (ll. 25–28)

He has already felt the "sweet influences" (l. 21) of nature—the "singing lark," the "vernal corn-field," "the level sunshine" that "glimmers with green light" (ll. 7–20)— and his spirit has drunk in its joy, but he sees them only as ministering to his escape from the world.

But as the poet's mind turns to the world outside this silent place, melancholy descends upon him like a weight:

> O my God!
> It weighs upon the heart, that he must think
> What uproar and what strife may now be stirring
> This way or that way o'er these silent hills.
> (ll. 32–35)

The "small and silent dell" is an escape from the world, but not a legitimate escape for the man of conscience. The effect of the hundred and fifty lines that follow—often moving in the depth and intensity of their feeling—is to allow the larger world of human society, torn by violence, to press in on this sequestered little world the poet has found. What he comes to learn is that there is an intrinsic relationship between this silent valley and the great world outside, a relationship that, for him, is mediated by England herself:

> O native Britain! O my Mother Isle!
> . . . .
> There lives nor form nor feeling in my soul
> Unborrowed from my country!
> (ll. 182–93)

Both the "sweet influences" of nature and his just anger at England's enemies are owed to her, and the two feelings cannot be separated.

In the same moment of this realization, too, the poet comes to another perception—of the working of God in and through his native land:

> O my Mother Isle!
> How shouldst thou prove aught else but dear and holy
> To me, who from thy lakes and mountain-hills,
> Thy clouds, thy quiet dales, thy rocks and seas,

Have drunk in all my intellectual life,
All sweet sensations, all ennobling thoughts,
All adoration of the God in nature,
All lovely and all honourable things,
Whatever makes this mortal spirit feel
The joy and greatness of its future being?
                   . . . O divine
And beauteous island! thou hast been my sole
And most magnificent temple, in the which
I walk with awe, and sing my stately songs,
Loving the God that made me!

                            (ll. 182–97)

He has, for the moment, glimpsed the *natura naturans,* the active principle that is at work to make his beloved England what it is—and that "makes this mortal spirit feel / The joy and greatness of its future being."

The role of joy in this complex equation has been a curious one. Joy makes its presence felt early in the poem, as the poet listens in his "small and silent dell" to the singing lark "that sings unseen / The minstrelsy that solitude loves best" (ll. 18–19). Under the "sweet influences" of nature, he experiences "a meditative joy" (l. 23), which is (as not infrequently in Coleridge) associated with religious feelings: "and found / Religious meanings in the forms of Nature" (ll. 23–24). His joy is premature, however, because—as we have seen—it brings and reflects not an intense union with reality but a dreamlike state of being: "In a half sleep, he dreams of better worlds" (l. 26). The result, therefore, is a sharp decline into melancholy, as he recalls how the larger world outside this silent dell threatens uproar and strife. That destructive world of society, where the threatened invasion of England is brewing, counterfeits joy in its perversion of religious faith:

All, all make up one scheme of perjury,
That faith doth reel; the very name of God
Sounds like a juggler's charm; and, bold with joy,
                     . . . the owlet Atheism,
Sailing on obscene wings athwart the noon,
Drops his blue-fringéd lids, and holds them close,
And hooting at the glorious sun in Heaven,
Cries out, 'Where is it?'

                            (ll. 78–86)

As this is false religion, so is this false joy, founded not on love but on hatred.

It is only through the process of exorcising, as it were, these demons of hatred by telling the truth about them ("I have told / Most bitter truth, but without bitterness," ll. 154–55) that true joy can reach him. It is only when he comes to perceive not only nature but also the bonds that exist between nature and England and all those dear to him ("All bonds of natural love," l. 180) that he experiences "All sweet sensations, all ennobling thoughts, / All adoration of the God in nature" (ll. 187–88)—and that his spirit feels "The joy and greatness of its future being" (l. 191).

Now the poet is no longer dreaming in the green and silent dell. His two perceptions, of the still peace of the little valley and of the war-torn world outside, are no longer separate. There can be, and must be, communion between them. As he emerges from the dell and follows the green sheep-track "up the heathy hill" (l. 209), we are not surprised to see him on the brow of the hill gazing out over the fields toward the sea, with a larger view to match his enlarged inner vision. The world of nature and the world of human society can now meet, and in this meeting there is hope:

> And after lonely sojourning
> In such a quiet and surrounded nook,
> This burst of prospect, here the shadowy main,
> Dim-tinted, there the mighty majesty
> Of that huge amphitheatre of rich
> And elmy fields, seems like society—
> Conversing with the mind, and giving it
> A livelier impulse and a dance of thought!
>   (ll. 213–20)

With this larger view, and with his conscience more at rest, the poet can return to his friend and to his wife and child with a sense that his heart is more worthy "to indulge / Love, and the thoughts that yearn for human kind" (ll. 231–32).

* * *

In "The Nightingale," the last poem we shall consider, we find the same pattern, but here developed lyrically rather than dramatically. That is to say, the poet undergoes no "conversion" from preoccupation with self to openness of heart. The poet's realization of his harmony with nature is essentially the same at the end as at the beginning; it is simply deepened and expanded through the experience of the poem. What the poem allows us to see is the foundation of his perception: how his perception is grounded in an encounter, through nature, with the "pure principle of Love."

From the very outset of the poem, there are no misgivings, no doubts; there is no sense of unexpressed limitations. The poet is in tune with the natural world around him: although the stars are dim, the thought of fruitful showers allows him to find "a pleasure in the dimness of the stars" (l. 11). He is at one and at ease with his companions: "Come, we will rest on this old mossy bridge!" (l. 4). From the outset, too, there is joy: the showers "gladden the green earth" (l. 10), and the nightingale, for all the mistaken notions about him among melancholy young poets, is the "merry Nightingale" (l. 43). The poet and his friends have no trouble affirming that "Nature's sweet voices" are "always full of love / And joyance" (ll. 42–43).

Not less important, the poet is self-confident about his poetic vocation: he can smile, self-assuredly, at the poor poet who hears the nightingale's song as melancholy. He knows, with a sure instinct, what it is a poet must do—open himself to the influences of nature:

> to the influxes
> Of shapes and sounds and shifting elements
> Surrendering his whole spirit, of his song
> And of his fame forgetful! so his fame
> Should share in Nature's immortality,
> A venerable thing! and so his song
> Should make all Nature lovelier, and itself
> Be loved like Nature!
>
> (ll. 27–34)

He already knows that a poet, if he is to fulfill his mission, must allow the active principle of nature to work in him, and what the rest of the poem shows us is how it *happens* to him on this balmy evening as he listens to the song of the nightingale.

It happens, curiously, as he tells a snatch of story about a grove, "hard by a castle huge" (l. 50), where nightingales sing. As he tells the story, the natural beauty he describes more and more takes possession of him, as he hears the birds "answer and provoke each other's song" (l. 58), until at last he hears

> one low piping sound more sweet than all—
> Stirring the air with such a harmony,
> That should you close your eyes, you might almost
> Forget it was not day!
>
> (ll. 61–64)

The gentle Maid, who "knows all their notes, / That gentle Maid!" (ll. 74–75), is vowed to "something more than Nature in the grove" (l. 73). As he is drawn more and more deeply into the experience of sights and sounds he is describing—of brightness and half-light, of a symphony of sounds—the poet suddenly (through the Maid) hears "a pause of silence,"

> till the moon
> Emerging, hath awakened earth and sky
> With one sensation, and those wakeful birds
> Have all burst forth in choral minstrelsy,
> As if some sudden gale had swept at once
> A hundred airy harps!
>
> (ll. 77–82)

It is once again, of course, "the one Life within us and abroad," and once again—mediated through the Maid and through the poet's experience of her natural world—it puts the poet in touch with the very principle of nature itself, "something more than Nature in the grove."

This "vision" is clearly a joyful union, too, and the joyous nightingales singled out at the end of that vision perhaps suggest the poet himself, that other singer of songs, and his whole tribe of joyful poets:

And she hath watched
Many a nightingale perch giddily
On blossomy twig still swinging from the breeze,
And to that motion tune his wanton song
Like tipsy Joy that reels with tossing head.

(ll. 82–86)

Here are the real poets, not the melancholy indoor youths who counterfeit poetic feeling, but the poets who "tune their wanton song" to the motions of nature, the "blossomy twig still swinging from the breeze." Only in tune with nature's song can there be true joy: "Nature's sweet voices, always full of love / And joyance."

Touched by the Spirit of nature, through the nightingale's song, the poet can return home resolved in heart that his child shall know what he has known:

if that Heaven
Should give me life, his childhood shall grow up
Familiar with these songs, that with the night
He may associate joy.

(ll. 106–9)

To return once more to our opening passage from Wordsworth: having experienced "love and joyance" in the purity of nature,

he cannot chuse
But seek for objects of a kindred Love
In fellow-natures, & a kindred Joy.

It is no wonder George McLean Harper calls these "Poems of Friendship," for they are set against the background of Coleridge's enormous capacity for friendship and his urgent need for the support of friends. But at the same time these poems are so much more: they are about the very nature of love. If we take account of their beginning and ending, as we customarily do, we can see the beauty of their shape, the lovely curve of going out and return—the movement by which the poet's love is deepened and enlarged through the working of his sympathetic imagination. If we allow ourselves to be drawn into the process by which the poet enters, in imagination, into the life of nature and of his friends, we ourselves share, vicariously, in this imaginative and liberating act of love. But if we also take account of the poet's encounter with the very power of nature itself, the *natura naturans,* the active principle by which nature pours itself out in the world—the very Spirit of nature—then we may experience, with the poet, something even more: the foundation, the source, the "pure principle of Love." Having experienced this, one can know even more deeply what it is to turn to one's fellow men and women and find love echoed there:

his thoughts now flowing clear
From a clear fountain flowing, he looks round—
He seeks for Good & finds the Good he seeks.

Fear at my heart, as at a cup,
My life-blood seemed to sip!

* * *

I looked to heaven, and tried to pray;
But or ever a prayer had gusht,
A wicked whisper came, and made
My heart as dry as dust.

* * *

A spring of love gushed from my heart,
And I blessed them unaware.

* * *

Since then, at an uncertain hour,
That agony returns:
And till my ghastly tale is told,
This heart within me burns.

— *"The Rime of the Ancient Mariner"*

CHAPTER 4

"The Rime of the Ancient Mariner":

"This Heart within Me Burns"

Contemplating Gustave Doré's stirring engravings of "The Rime of the Ancient Mariner"—the dark terror of the strange forces that grip the Mariner and his ship, the sea bright with unearthly light, the nightmare vision of the ghostly figures casting dice for the Mariner's soul, the beauty of the seraphic creatures—one can readily believe the long-accepted orthodoxy that this is indeed a "supernatural" poem. However, it was one of the many contributions of the late George Whalley to Coleridge studies, as long ago as forty years, to underscore for us the centrality of human feeling in the poem.[1]

To begin with, Whalley cites no less an authority than Charles Lamb, who wrote in a letter to Wordsworth in 1801: "For me, I was never so affected with any human Tale. After first reading it, I was totally possessed by it for many days—I dislike all the miraculous part of it, but the feelings of the man under the operation of such scenery dragged me along like Tom Piper's magic whistle."[2] For Whalley, the "haunting quality" of the poem comes, not so much from the supernatural and nightmare qualities of the poem, as from "our intimate experience in the poem of the most intense personal suffering, perplexity, loneliness, longing, horror, fear."[3] It is, in short, the *human* dimensions of the poem, not the incursions from a supernatural world, that affect us most profoundly.

I too would like to argue that, however much "The Rime of the Ancient Mariner" may be about a supernatural experience—as of course it is—it is equally as much about human feeling, even including something as basic as the "domestic affections." I suggest that what Morris Dickstein said of the conversation poems is equally true of the "Ancient Mariner." Here too "Coleridge's deepest impulse is to reconcile the visionary imagination with ordinary human bonds, with family and domesticity, with

---

1. See "The Mariner and the Albatross," in *Coleridge: A Collection of Critical Essays,* ed. Kathleen Coburn, pp. 32–33.

2. *Letters of Charles and Mary Lamb,* ed. E. V. Lucas, 1:240; quoted by Whalley, "The Mariner and the Albatross," p. 32.

3. "The Mariner and the Albatross," p. 33.

love, with social benevolence."[4] Here we may also find, though of course in a much more complex way, the same pattern as in the conversation poems: movement from a limited experience of love, through an encounter with the *natura naturans*—the active powers of nature—to a deeper experience of the meaning of love. Here, however, the lesson will be a much more costly one.

* * *

As the Mariner looks back on his experience, he pictures himself as happy enough at the beginning of his adventure:

> The ship was cheered, the harbour cleared,
> Merrily did we drop
> Below the kirk, below the hill,
> Below the lighthouse top.
>
> (ll. 21–24)

He was part of a cheerful band of sailors, who sailed forth eagerly with all the world before them. They were clearly a "company," a group to whom one's identity could be subordinated. It is perhaps significant, as Richard Haven has pointed out, that the Mariner uses the pronoun *we* throughout part I; it is only in the last line that he sets himself apart from his shipmates, saying "I shot the ALBATROSS" (l. 82). As Haven puts it, "It is with his unmotivated, inexplicable act of violence that he becomes a self-conscious individual rather than a social unit."[5]

At first glance, it might seem that the Mariner has passed from human fellowship to self-centeredness, thus losing touch with human community. But consider the company from which he has withdrawn: a band of undifferentiated men who have themselves withdrawn from ordinary human society—leaving home, church, and the safe harbor of their "own countree." There is no evidence that they are really a "community"; on the face of things, at least, they are simply a "group," from whom the Mariner has distanced himself by acting independently. Yet, at the same time, if the Mariner has gained independence from this undifferentiated group, he has also lost something: a location in the world, as it were, a place to stand. As Haven succinctly expresses it, "he is part of nothing."[6] From this point on, through much of the poem, the Mariner experiences "aloneness." It is not solitude—"that solitude which suits / Abstruser musings"—but loneliness.

What the Mariner is searching for, I suggest, is what anyone is seeking who leaves home: his place in the world. He is looking for his "own countree," his true "home," even as Coleridge himself did all his life. This is, I believe, a central force in the poem: the tension in the Mariner between the aloneness he feels and the home he longs for, a place where he "belongs."

---

4. "Coleridge, Wordsworth, and the 'Conversation Poems,'" p. 374.
5. *Patterns of Consciousness: An Essay on Coleridge*, p. 29.
6. Ibid., p. 30.

However, even as the Mariner sets himself apart from his shipmates by shooting the albatross, he finds that they in turn have rejected him:

> Ah! well a-day! what evil looks
> Had I from old and young!
> (ll. 139–40)

Thrown back on himself, cut off from all human community, he sees the skeleton ship and the nightmare vision of Life-in-Death. In such a world, there is no room for love in his heart; there is only fear—of aloneness and of strange powers beyond his knowing. If the scriptural injunction is true, that "perfect love casteth out fear" (1 John 4:18), perhaps it is also true that fear casts out love—for clearly it is fear that here drains dry his heart:

> Fear at my heart, as at a cup,
> My life-blood seemed to sip!
> (ll. 204–5)

Obviously his fear is justified, for immediately afterward Death claims his spoils—the Mariner's comrades:

> One after one, by the star-dogged Moon,
> Too quick for groan or sigh,
> Each turned his face with a ghastly pang,
> And cursed me with his eye.
>
> Four times fifty living men,
> (And I heard nor sigh nor groan)
> With heavy thump, a lifeless lump,
> They dropped down one by one.
> (ll. 212–19)

Now the Mariner is truly alone, reaching in fact the nadir of his isolation:

> Alone, alone, all, all alone,
> Alone on a wide wide sea!
> And never a saint took pity on
> My soul in agony.
> (ll. 232–35)

Love has now completely left him:

> I looked to heaven, and tried to pray;
> But or ever a prayer had gusht,
> A wicked whisper came, and made
> My heart as dry as dust.
> (ll. 244–47)

What is the "wicked whisper"? Since it comes as he tries to pray, and since it is a "wicked" whisper, we may reasonably conjecture that it is something like the traditional voice of the tempting spirit, taunting him with the ultimate temptation—despair—telling him that he is now utterly alone, that even God has left him.

This "dryness of heart" does not remain long with the Mariner, however, for it is only a few lines later that he *does* pray, when a "spring of love" gushes from his heart and he blesses the water snakes, whereupon the albatross falls from his neck (ll. 284–91). How to explain this remarkable change, so swift, so dramatic? Consider what has intervened between the moment when his heart was as "dry as dust" (l. 247) and this climactic moment when the "spring of love" gushes from his heart (l. 284). A vision has come to him—and with this vision new perception—as he becomes aware of the beneficent moon, which is as calm as he is tortured:

> The moving Moon went up the sky,
> And no where did abide:
> Softly she was going up,
> And a star or two beside—
>
> (ll. 263–66)

It is as if this quiet scene, in such sharp contrast with his agonized spirit, calms his soul, so that he can allow its gentle influence to flow into him. Out of this calm communion with the beauty of the "moving Moon," he finds himself in touch with the very principle of nature itself, the dynamic power of process—the *natura naturans* revealing itself through the *natura naturata:*

> Beyond the shadow of the ship,
> I watched the water-snakes:
> They moved in tracks of shining white,
> And when they reared, the elfish light
> Fell off in hoary flakes.
>
> Within the shadow of the ship
> I watched their rich attire:
> Blue, glossy green, and velvet black,
> They coiled and swam; and every track
> Was a flash of golden fire.
>
> (ll. 272–81)[7]

7. Patrick Kelly has argued persuasively that the vision of the water snakes is really a vision of the "art of God": "The snakes within the shadow of the ship are an abridgement of nature—a part of nature that is humanized. But it is not merely the Mariner's love that humanizes them. That love is made possible by the ship and the moon which conspire to form the shadow that gives order to a small part of the silent sea. The ship, I would suggest, is the type of art at this point in the poem and the moon, the type of God's imagination—the source of the human imagination for Coleridge." This "aesthetic perception of the snakes within the shadow of the ship has a spiritual validity: the human capacity to perceive beauty in this shadowy existence on earth is an intimation of immortality" ("Day and Night: Mystery and Error in Coleridge's 'The Rime of the Ancient Mariner,'" pp. 303, 305). I would add that the love the Mariner feels, therefore, is love not merely of the *natura naturata* but also of the *natura naturans,* not only of the beauty he sees but also of the source of beauty.

Now what had been ugly ("slimy things did crawl with legs / Upon the slimy sea," ll. 125–26) can be seen in its true beauty:

> O happy living things! no tongue
> Their beauty might declare:
> A spring of love gushed from my heart,
> And I blessed them unaware:
> Sure my kind saint took pity on me,
> And I blessed them unaware.
>
> (ll. 282–87)

This vision, which brings the Mariner to a fresh perception of the world, is pure gift, from a power beyond himself—yet it appears within him. He has done nothing to earn it; he is not even aware of its coming. It is simply given to him, in this respect much like Wordsworth's vision on Mount Snowdon: "that vision, given to spirits of the night / And three chance human wanderers."[8]

The gratuity of this new vision is, I believe, of crucial significance. What it implies is that, in the depth of his despair, love can come to him only by grace. His will is, for the moment at least, of no use to him; only an act of grace can renew his spirit, can turn the dryness of his heart to a "spring of love." Only a blessing from above can enable the Mariner to become in turn a source of blessing for others. As Anthony Harding says,

> It is not the recipients of the blessing who are important, but its divine origin, and the fact that the 'spring of love' enables the Marinere to transcend his selfhood for the first time. It does not matter whether the object of his love is water-snakes, stars or Polar Spirits; the important thing is that God, acting perhaps through some 'kind saint', has made the Marinere's self a centre and source instead of an enclosing and defensive wall.[9]

The Mariner, opened by the touch of God's love, can perceive the world around him with newly awakened senses. Awaking from the "gentle sleep" (l. 295) that followed his release from the burden of the albatross, he is granted a further vision, the "troop of spirits blest" (l. 349) and their symphony of "sweet sounds" (ll. 347–72). Under this beneficent influence, the ship "quietly sailed on" (l. 373).

We soon learn, however, that this incursion of divine grace into the Mariner's soul is not enough, for now the ship becomes agitated once again:

> But in a minute she 'gan stir,
> With a short uneasy motion—
> Backwards and forwards half her length
> With a short uneasy motion.
>
> Then like a pawing horse let go,
> She made a sudden bound:

8. *The Prelude* (1850), 14. 64–65.
9. *Coleridge and the Idea of Love: Aspects of Relationship in Coleridge's Thought and Writing,* p. 63.

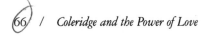

It flung the blood into my head,
And I fell down in a swound.

(ll. 385–92)

Two mysterious voices then make it clear that the Mariner still has far to go:

'The man hath penance done
And penance more will do.'

(ll. 408–9)

What remains to him involves, at least in part, the exercise of his will. Love could not originate with him, for God is the source of love, but it must not end with him. He must learn, through the long journey of his life, to exercise the gift of love he has been given. This is the traditional way of the saints, and indeed the way to which all Christian pilgrims are called: to accept God's grace and to exercise it in loving charity.

(Theologically, the conception is eminently orthodox: both God and man must be active in the work of salvation.)The belief that God is constantly active in the world he has created, maintaining it in existence by his continuing presence, is the traditional teaching of all the Schoolmen, and indeed of patristic theology before them. "If God did not continue to be creatively present to all creation (the medieval Scholastic term for this active presence is 'conservatio'), creation would simply cease to be." But since Coleridge always assumes a connaturality between the divine and human minds (imagination is, after all, a "repetition in the finite mind of the eternal act of creation"), the human being has a further privileged relationship with God: "Present to all creation, God is present in a special way to the intelligent beings of his creation in their free actions; by this presence, this 'concursus divinus' (as the Scholastics called it), God's creative mind and will are united to man's."[10]

Coleridge's idea of "translucence" may be useful here. A symbol (the product of imagination) is characterized, Coleridge wrote, "above all by a translucence of the Eternal in and through the Temporal. It always partakes of the Reality which it renders intelligible; and while it enunciates the whole, abides itself as a living part in that Unity, of which it is the representative."[11] Symbol, therefore, "expresses not merely the juxtaposition of two realities (as metaphor can do) but articulates, however dimly, the 'interpenetration' of two disparate and often seemingly distant realities, such as man and God. It is by such language—poetic language—that the chasm between the immanent and the transcendent can be bridged."[12] The symbolic actions of the Mariner are just such realities, for the human action (such as the blessing of the water snakes) not only points to transcendent reality but actually "partakes of the Reality which it renders intelligible." Thus, as the theologians insist, each free action—at once free and graced by God—may be said to be wholly man's action and wholly God's, for (in Coleridge's terms) the two realities have "interpenetrated."

10. J. Robert Barth, S.J., "Theological Implications of Coleridge's Theory of Imagination," p. 24.
11. *LS*, p. 30.
12. Barth, "Theological Implications of Coleridge's Theory of Imagination," p. 29.

Thus the call to the Mariner is to allow this dual reality to work in him: to accept the help of God's grace and to exercise it freely in love; to act lovingly, so constantly and consistently that love at last becomes a "habit of the soul." Harding expresses the idea eloquently: Christian charity involves, he says, "a permanent effort to realign the deepest human feelings, so that acts of charity stem from him as naturally as fruit or flowers from a plant, and to reshape the consciousness of self, so that the self is no longer exclusive but inclusive, and radiates the love whose origin is found in God alone."[13]

The Mariner has not yet reached that state of perfection, but he is at least ready to return to human society, to continue his pilgrimage among his fellow human beings. For what has been revealed to him is the potential for love within himself and others; although the ultimate source of love is not himself, he has felt love spring up within him. His mission, then, will be to work out his salvation by sharing with others the love he has received. He must return from the visionary world of the spirits to the workaday world of family, friends, church, and society—in short, the world of the "domestic affections" and of societal responsibility.

> Oh! dream of joy! is this indeed
> The light-house top I see?
> Is this the hill? is this the kirk?
> Is this mine own countree?
> (ll. 464–67)

This is a return, to be sure, but it is a return in the spirit of T. S. Eliot at the end of "Little Gidding," involving a new perception of himself and of "home":

> And the end of all our exploring
> Will be to arrive where we started
> And know the place for the first time.[14]

The problem is, however, that although the Mariner has reached home at last, he cannot remain there. He cannot be permanently "home," because he has discovered a world of reality beyond; he is divided in consciousness, for he now realizes that he "belongs" in both worlds. John Beer suggests very tellingly that "fallen humanity cannot bear the revelation of infinity: and the Ancient Mariner, by breaking through the veils of convention and custom with which mankind normally defends itself from the unbearable supernatural, has brought upon himself the curse of Cain."[15] I suggest, however, that the Mariner's experience of infinity has been more complex than this. He has indeed experienced the terror of the infinite. One need only recall, for example, the Mariner's vision of the Sun as it shone above the spectre-ship:

13. *Coleridge and the Idea of Love*, p. 61.
14. *Four Quartets*, p. 48.
15. *Coleridge the Visionary*, p. 165.

And straight the Sun was flecked with bars,
(Heaven's Mother send us grace!)
As if through a dungeon-grate he peered
With broad and burning face.

(ll. 177–80)

The Mariner is here experiencing an infinity of hell, imaged as imprisonment in a dungeon of fire. It is no wonder that in this context he exclaims: "Fear at my heart as at a cup, / My life-blood seemed to sip!" He has experienced, too, infinity as dereliction—another dimension of hell:

Alone, alone, all, all alone,
Alone on a wide wide sea!
And never a saint took pity on
My soul in agony.

(ll. 232–35)

Even more terrifying, of course, was the original version in *Lyrical Ballads*—"And Christ would take no pity on / My soul in agony"—for there it was the Redeemer himself who seemed to abandon him. The Mariner's retrospective glance just before the end of the poem expresses this same sense of abandonment even by God:

O Wedding-Guest! this soul hath been
Alone on a wide wide sea:
So lonely 'twas, that God himself
Scarce seeméd there to be.

(ll. 597–600)

God can seem merciless, at certain moments in the history of a soul, when he reveals to the sinner his own sin and emptiness; and surely the Mariner has experienced this ruthless revelation—the revelation of the pitiless Sun beating down on the endless sea.

But, if the Mariner has experienced the dark side of infinity, he has also felt its merciful kindness: gentle sleep (ll. 292–96); the blessing of rain (ll. 299–304); the beautiful sounds of the "troop of spirits blest":

Around, around, flew each sweet sound,
Then darted to the Sun;
Slowly the sounds came back again,
Now mixed, now one by one.

Sometimes a-dropping from the sky
I heard the sky-lark sing;
Sometimes all little birds that are,
How they seemed to fill the sea and air
With their sweet jargoning!

And now 'twas like all instruments,
Now like a lonely flute;

And now it is an angel's song,
That makes the heavens be mute.
                    (ll. 354–66)

The Sun that had been terrifying is now (l. 355) a focal point of gracious blessing. The divine has two faces—a face of terror and a face of love. Mankind cannot look, with naked eyes, on God: "thou canst not see my face: for there shall no man see me, and live" (Exodus 33:20). But at times—in chosen times, to chosen people—God shows himself hidden behind a veil: the *natura naturans* revealing itself through the *natura naturata*. Here God reveals himself to the Mariner through the sounds of the troop of blessed spirits. At other moments he reveals himself through the Sun's reflected light, that of the Moon—gentler, more accommodated to human sight.

The moving Moon went up the sky,
And no where did abide:
Softly she was going up,
And a star or two beside—
                    (ll. 263–66)

The Sun is pitiless, revealing all—even the Mariner's innermost emptiness; the Moon is gracious, allowing him to breathe awhile, granting him "the gentle sleep from Heaven" under the loving hand of "Mary Queen" (ll. 294–95), who herself images God's graciousness rather than his ruthless purity of being.

It has often been pointed out that the imagery of Sun and Moon in the poem is not perfectly consistent. Perhaps what we have said suggests the reason. God cannot be perfectly imaged: what we perceive as cruelty may be actually an aspect of his love, demanding of us that we become our own best selves—sometimes even at great cost—much as the fugitive in Francis Thompson's "Hound of Heaven" recoils from his divine pursuer's hand, not recognizing that it is "outstretched caressingly." The Sun may seem at times unpitying, but it is the source of all light—including the gentle light of the Moon—and of all life.

John Beer's perceptive comment might, therefore, be qualified. It is indeed true that "fallen humanity cannot bear the revelation of infinity," at least not in its naked purity. However, it does not necessarily follow that the Mariner, having glimpsed the terror of the divine, "has brought upon himself the curse of Cain." Perhaps he has simply become a "pilgrim" in the long Christian tradition, who has come to know that "we have not here a lasting city," that the Christian is called to live in this world with the realization that his true "home" is in a world beyond. If the Mariner is a more literal wanderer than most, it is because he also stands in the ancient line of the prophets, who see more clearly the truths most of us try to forget.

*   *   *

Although the Mariner's return to his "own countree" may not be permanent, one thing that seems to be more lasting is his conversion of heart. First beset by fear, indeed drained of its very life by his terror of unknown powers ("Fear at my heart, as at a cup, / My life-blood seemed to sip"), the Mariner's heart becomes "as dry as dust," as he yields to despair. A gratuitous gift of grace, however, brings a spring of love to his heart, even as, shortly after, the welcome rain falls on his parched body. The ecstatic joy that accompanied the "spring of love"—"O happy living things! No tongue / Their beauty might declare"—was not to last, of course, but his heart was to remain thereafter alive. Just as the heart can be alive to joy, it can also be alive to sorrow or pain. As his journey on the sea was an experience of both terror and joy—of both the fear and the love of the transcendent—so his wandering life on earth will be made up of pain and happiness. There will be moments when he can "walk together to the kirk / With a goodly company" (ll. 603–4)—for " 'Tis sweeter far to me" (l. 602)—but there will be other moments when the "penance of life" will fall upon him once again:

> Since then, at an uncertain hour,
> That agony returns:
> And till my ghastly tale is told,
> This heart within me burns.
> (ll. 582–85)

We are led to suppose that—as in his first recounting of his story to the hermit—once his tale has been told, he is free of his burden until his heart again burns within him:

> Forthwith this frame of mine was wrenched
> With a woful agony,
> Which forced me to begin my tale;
> And then it left me free.
> (ll. 578–81)

We do the Mariner an unkindness, I believe, if we imagine him roaming the world in constant agony. It is true, of course, that his extraordinary experience gives him particularly onerous responsibilities; he is, after all, a prophet, burdened with special gifts. At the same time, though, he is one of us—in Wordsworth's phrase from the Preface to *Lyrical Ballads,* "a man speaking to men." His life, therefore, like ours, is compounded of sorrow and joy: moments of alienation and moments of sharing, days when his heart "within him burns" and days when he feels the sweetness of human communion.

➤ This renewal of the Mariner's heart is, I have argued, a gratuitous gift of God. If a "spring of love" rises up in the Mariner's heart, it is clear that its ultimate source is an ever-flowing fountain. John Beer has called attention to the fountain imagery (with its obvious debt to the Neoplatonic image of the "burning fountain," which Coleridge knew not only directly from Proclus but also indirectly from his study of Jakob Boehme) that is implicit in the lovely vision of the blessed spirits (ll. 350–66), where the Sun seems not only the focal point but also the source of all this beauty, life, and love:

Around, around, flew each sweet sound,
Then darted to the Sun;
Slowly the sounds came back again,
Now mixed, now one by one.

This insight, about the relationship between the spring and the fountain, Beer sees as very close to the central significance of the poem: "The core of the poem, on this interpretation, consists of a series of experiences which are closely related to the view of humanity . . . developed from Boehme and the Neoplatonists: a view whereby human beings find their true home in the universe only when they are able to perceive the correspondence between the spring-like heart of man and the fountainous heart of nature."[16] I would add that the nature represented by the fountain is for Coleridge the *natura naturans,* the principle and source of all life and all love. Both the sweetness and the "burning" the Mariner feels in his heart flow from this "burning fountain." Since the spring of his heart is fed by this fountain, he can walk in its strength—in suffering and in joy—for the rest of his life.

*   *   *

Like Coleridge himself, the Mariner is on an endless search for home, for a place where he "belongs": whether it be a literal home, or the heart's home in some other world where all one's longings will be fulfilled. Each of these possible meanings of "home" is underscored by one of the two "frames" in which Coleridge sets the Mariner's story.

The first of these, the longing for hearth and home and the domestic affections, is emphasized by the striking frame of the wedding feast in which Coleridge sets the Mariner's tale. This is a celebration of life and love and the establishment of a home, where both life and love will be nurtured. One has the sense that the Mariner is drawn ineluctably to this celebration, wanting to be part of it yet not being able to be. He is drawn to it because it represents a need of his soul, yet he cannot enter in because his soul has found an even greater need. He can enter the church, where the blessing of heaven is given to human love, but he cannot share in the joyful human festivities:

O sweeter than the marriage-feast,
'Tis sweeter far to me,
To walk together to the kirk
With a goodly company!
                    (ll. 601–4)

What of the wedding guest? Is it significant that the object of the Mariner's attention is not one of the principals of the wedding—the bride or groom—but one of the guests? Since he is not accompanied by a spouse, we may infer that the guest has not yet himself married. He is in a middle state between the Mariner and the newly

16. *Wordsworth and the Human Heart,* p. 58.

married couple. The husband and wife have committed themselves to human love and a life of domesticity, making it more difficult (at least on the face of it) for them to experience the larger world the Mariner has encountered; their comfortable domestic love might protect them from the terrors of the larger mysteries beyond. The Mariner, however much he may long for such a refuge, cannot have it. The wedding guest, however, is in a perilous state between, uncommitted, still open to the dangerous potentialities offered to him by the Mariner's tale.

In a sense, this is admittedly a somewhat dichotomous view, as if the Mariner's knowledge of the deeper mysteries is incompatible with the comfortable affections of hearth and home. But for the Mariner this may indeed be the case. He is, after all, a prophet figure, the one who carries, often reluctantly, the burden of special revelation and the social responsibility it calls for; he is thus bound to his community by a special bond, yet alienated from it by his pain and his knowledge of mysteries his companions can only glimpse. The wedding guest represents a potential bridge between these two worlds of knowledge and experience. Still uncommitted, he is free to hear the Mariner's unsettling words and carry them in his heart, as indeed he does:

A sadder and a wiser man,
He rose the morrow morn.
(ll. 624–25)

When at last he comes to his own wedding day, he will bring with him the glimpse he has had of another world. He will know that domestic love—and the pains and mysteries that go with it—is not all; that there are still possibilities of other and even deeper experience, both of joy and of pain, other mysteries to be explored.

* * *

Sometime before the publication of *Sibylline Leaves* in 1816, Coleridge added still another frame to his poem: the fascinating prose gloss, written in the form of a commentary by an editor from an earlier age, so that the poem becomes (in John Beer's words) "a fiction which is not only related by a fictitious hero but commented upon by a fictitious editor."[17] Views of this gloss vary considerably, from annoyance at what seems its intrusiveness to celebration of its eloquent appropriateness. George Watson suggests that "the purpose and effect of the gloss can only be to intensify the historical, dramatic, 'as-if' element in the poem. . . . Its effect is deliberately to enlarge doubt concerning what the Mariner says, to remind the reader that . . . the poem is an historical exercise which asks not to be taken literally. Coleridge, in a manner almost too ingenious, has on this occasion insisted that we should feel the gap of centuries."[18] Thus, in this reading, we are further distanced by the gloss from the life of the poem.

For Richard Haven, however, the gloss has quite another effect: It distances us, not from the action of the poem, but from our natural desire for rational explanation. Of

17. Coleridge, *Poems,* ed. John Beer, Introduction, p. xviii.
18. *Coleridge the Poet,* p. 93.

the action of the poem itself, Haven notes: "Intensely present, the events are vaguely remote from our normal frame of reference. Because we do not know where we are, we do not know what labels we should apply. We are therefore forced, again like the Wedding Guest, simply to watch and listen." The gloss, he continues, is "a further step in this artful isolation of the experience from rationalization and explanation." It is "one more voice, one more frame, a circle at one more remove from the immediate 'facts' which are presented to us. The gloss seems like a commentary, but it provides a psychological rather than a rational satisfaction. Our questions are answered with learned allusions to Michael Psellus or the Jew Josephus, and we accept, our disbelief transmuted for the moment into faith."[19]

The kind of "faith" to which the reader is called by the gloss is quite different from that of the wedding frame. The call there was to faith in the domestic affections represented by the marriage, underscoring the Mariner's longing for his own home: his native town, his "own countree." The frame provided by the prose gloss calls us to believe in another "home"—that home the Mariner longs for in a land beyond, in the mysterious world he has discovered in the course of his strange voyage, where he has experienced so much pain and yet so much beauty and love. This is the realm of the spirits, where (in the scriptural phrase) "they neither marry, nor are given in marriage; but are as the angels which are in heaven" (Mark 12:25).

The gloss by the learned "editor" begins, I suggest, with the Latin epigraph adapted from Thomas Burnet. It was added at the same time as the gloss and, like the gloss, is scholarly in tone, is drawn from learned authority, and is preoccupied with the mysteries of the unknown.

> Facile credo, plures esse Naturas invisibiles quam visibiles in rerum universitate. Sed horum omnium familiam quis nobis enarrabit? et gradus et cognationes et discrimina et singulorum munera? Quid agunt? quae loca habitant? Harum rerum notitiam semper ambivit ingenium humanum, nunquam attigit. Juvat, interea, non diffiteor, quandoque in animo, tanquam in tabula, majoris et melioris mundi imaginem contemplari: ne mens assuefacta hodiernae vitae minutiis se contrahat nimis, et tota subsidat in pusillas cogitationes. Sed veritati interea invigilandum est, modusque servandus, ut certa ab incertis, diem a nocte, distinguamus.—T. Burnet, *Archaeol. Phil.* p. 68.[20]

Surely the Mariner has come to know "that there are more invisible than visible things in the universe" and has learned to give priority to the invisible.

It is instructive simply to read through the prose gloss consecutively, apart from the

---

19. *Patterns of Consciousness*, pp. 21–22.

20. Translation: "I readily believe that there are more invisible than visible things in the universe. But who shall describe for us their families, their ranks, relationships, distinguishing features and functions? What do they do? Where do they live? The human mind has always circled about knowledge of these things, but never attained it. I do not doubt, however, that it is sometimes good to contemplate in the mind, as in a picture, the image of a greater and better world; otherwise the intellect, habituated to the petty things of daily life, may too much contract itself, and wholly sink down to trivial thoughts. But meanwhile we must be vigilant for truth and keep proportion, that we may distinguish the certain from the uncertain, day from night" (translation from David Perkins, ed., *English Romantic Writers*, p. 405). The work of Burnet from which Coleridge is quoting is *Archaeologiae Philosophicae sive Doctrina Antiqua De Rerum Originibus* (1692).

poem. One quickly notices that there are only the most necessary references to the human actors in the drama. The attention of the commentator is primarily taken up with what represents the other world: the mysterious movements of the ship, the Polar-spirit and his fellow daemons, the skeleton-ship, the haunting figure of Life-in-Death, the guardian saint and the angelic spirits. In short, the editor seems to be interested above all in the supernatural world of mystery that has been revealed to the Mariner.

The editor's gloss reaches a climax of awe and celebration, at the midpoint of the poem, in the great vision of the "journeying Moon":

> In his loneliness and fixedness he yearneth towards the journeying Moon, and the stars that still sojourn, yet still move onward; and every where the blue sky belongs to them, and is their appointed rest, and their native country and their own natural homes, which they enter unannounced, as lords that are certainly expected and yet there is a silent joy at their arrival.[21]

Here is not only where the supernatural spirits have their "own natural homes"; it is also (although of course the Mariner himself can know this only by the longing in his spirit, his "burning heart") the Mariner's own destined home—unlike his "own countree" where he no longer belongs. This is for the Mariner, as we see by the reflected light of the editor's eloquent commentary, "the goal of all his striving." This is the hope that draws him on: not to return to "mine own countree," but to find at last his own true "natural home," where he too—like the spirits whose life he has come to share—can enter unannounced, as a lord that is "certainly expected," with silent joy at his coming.

* * *

We have seen that the Ancient Mariner has undergone a conversion of heart. However, as John Beer has pointed out, "when we look at the Mariner's final state . . . we see that it is not, as in the conventional story of conversion, that of a man who has moved from one state of consciousness to a happier one, in which he now feels himself more at home. On the contrary, he has become a perpetual wanderer." The Mariner has reached, though, one deep conviction. Through experiencing the ultimates of suffering and mental alienation, he has come to believe that the supreme accomplishment is to be found in the exercise of love." The expression of this belief as "He prayeth best, who loveth best" is not that of the poet (*his* formulation of it is the complex beauty of the poem) but that of the simple sailor. Thus this seemingly simplistic piety should be seen rather as a simple man's profound distillation of experience:

> Even the simplicity of the Mariner's final words to the Wedding-Guest has its model in religious tradition. It was said of the aged St John that when he grew too old to walk into

---

21. It has been noted what a perfect imitation this passage is of the prose of seventeenth-century divines like Jeremy Taylor; see Watson, *Coleridge the Poet,* p. 93. I might add how congruous the seventeenth-century Latin of Burnet is with the prose of the gloss.

assemblies of the faithful he would still be carried there, and that on such occasions he would give a single injunction, repeated over and over again: 'Little children, love one another.' So, it might be argued, the experiences of the wisest of the saints and those of a simple man exposed to the extremes of nature might in the end foster the same single condensation of wisdom.[22]

To this I would simply add that the Mariner has learned the importance not only of love but also of home, and has discovered how deeply the two depend on one another. Home is where one "belongs," where one is always forgiven—whatever the sin—and where love is not conditioned by one's merits or even by one's striving. No wonder these two wanderers, Coleridge and his Ancient Mariner, sought so longingly for home. For home is where the power of love dwells, whether it be the finite power we find in the human spirit and in human community or the fullness of power found only in divine transcendent reality—whether the "spring of love" or the burning fountain beyond.

22. John Beer, *Coleridge's Poetic Intelligence,* pp. 160–61.

All they who live in the upper sky,
Do love you, holy Christabel!

*   *   *

And what if in a world of sin
(O sorrow and shame should this be true!)
Such giddiness of heart and brain
Comes seldom save from rage and pain,
So talks as it's most used to do.

— *"Christabel"*

CHAPTER 5

"Christabel":

"What If in a World of Sin"

The old Latin tag is certainly applicable to "Christabel": *quot capita, tot sententiae.* There have indeed been, it sometimes seems, almost as many interpretations of the poem as there are interpreters. Part of the problem, no doubt, is its fragmentary state, which leaves unresolved most of the issues it raises. Recently, however, if there has not been agreement about its meaning, there has at least been some growing consensus about its general focus, for the more prevalent (and occasionally persuasive) readings involve Christabel's sexual initiation and her passage from innocence to experience.

One of the most convincing of these approaches, by Jonas Spatz, may be taken as fairly representative. Spatz sees Geraldine as a projection of Christabel's sexuality, "with its desire, fear, shame, and pleasure," which Christabel finds at once entrancing and repulsive. The poem therefore "traces its heroine's attempt to come to terms with her sexuality, to recognize its essential role in her love for her absent knight and in their approaching marriage, and to progress from adolescence to womanhood."[1] Such interpretations, and indeed most readings of the poem, invariably and naturally focus on the central relationship between Christabel and Geraldine. Without attempting a comprehensive reading of the poem, I would like to focus more closely than usual on a relationship that receives less attention, but which I believe is central to the poem's motive force: Christabel and her mother.

* * *

The poem introduces us, from the beginning, into a world where life is at a low ebb: in the dark of night the toothless bitch howls, seeing (some think) "my lady's shroud" (l. 13); the moon looks "both small and dull" (l. 19); and even the spring "comes slowly up this way" (l. 22). If the sense of life outside the castle is attenuated, the world inside offers even less, conveying in fact a distinct sense of death: the Baron's room is "as still as death" (l. 171); Christabel's mother, she tells us, "died the hour that I was born" (l.

1. Jonas Spatz, "Sexual Initiation in Coleridge's 'Christabel,'" p. 11. Gerald Enscoe has also written helpfully of Geraldine's role in Christabel's sexual initiation. If Geraldine is an "'evil' enchantress who, in a world picture dominated by the forces within the castle, is bent upon the destruction of innocence," she is at the same time "the personification of erotic, sexual forces entering the castle to perform their ministry through the seduction of Christabel" (*Eros and the Romantics: Sexual Love as a Theme in Coleridge, Shelley and Keats,* p. 45; see also pp. 36–60).

197); and the castle itself, as we see from the opening of part 2, has become almost a monument to the dead baroness, as the matin bell each morning "knells us back to a world of death" (l. 333).

In this strange atmosphere, where Geraldine seems an emissary from another world, where Christabel's mother is only a spirit, and where Sir Leoline has locked himself away from the world, only Christabel maintains a strong hold on life. It is significant that we first see Christabel in a natural setting, seemingly quite at home in the world of nature, where—however much it "comes slowly up this way"—the Spring still asserts its power of life. (Geraldine, on the contrary, seems out of place in the natural world: "I guess, 'twas frightful there to see / A lady so richly clad as she," ll. 66–67.) And Christabel is, alone in the poem—except perhaps for Bard Bracy—able to look to the future with hope:

> And she in the midnight wood will pray
> For the weal of her lover that's far away.
>   (ll. 29–30)

It is Christabel, too, who is capable of action: she can bring Geraldine into the castle and give her shelter, caring for her "in love and in charity." Even within the castle, she has access to the living powers of nature:

> I pray you, drink this cordial wine!
> It is a wine of virtuous powers;
> My mother made it of wild flowers.
>   (ll. 191–93)

Not least, Christabel is alive in that she has access to the world of prayer, both in the forest and within the castle. In short, whatever may later happen to her under the spell of Geraldine, Christabel's link with life is far stronger than that of any other figure in the poem.

But Christabel's hold on life seems very much bound up with her relationship with her mother. We might recall here Coleridge's belief that the primordial love is that of mother and child, and that all other relationships—whether human or divine—have their psychological beginnings in this relationship: "The first dawnings of [the infant's] humanity will break forth in the eye that connects the mother's face with the warmth of the mother's bosom. . . . Ere yet a conscious self exists the love begins, and the first love is love to an other."[2] It is no wonder then that we find Christabel, whose mother died in giving birth to her, longing for her presence; although she never felt "the warmth of the mother's bosom," clearly a deep bond of sympathy remains. Christabel says feelingly, for example:

> I have heard the grey-haired friar tell
> How on her death-bed she did say,

---

2. Quoted by John H. Muirhead, *Coleridge as Philosopher,* p. 252.

That she should hear the castle-bell
Strike twelve upon my wedding-day.
O mother dear! that thou wert here!
(ll. 198–202)

In the conclusion to part I, after Geraldine has held Christabel in her arms and now sleeps with her "as a mother with her child" (l. 301), we see Christabel smile in her sleep, "as infants at a sudden light!" (l. 318):

No doubt, she hath a vision sweet.
What if her guardian spirit 'twere,
What if she knew her mother near?
But this she knows, in joys and woes,
That saints will aid if men will call:
For the blue sky bends over all!
(ll. 326–31)

Christabel continues to be sustained by this vision, even as Sir Leoline embraces Geraldine, her seducer.

The touch, the sight, had passed away,
And in its stead that vision blest,
Which comforted her after-rest
While in the lady's arms she lay,
Had put a rapture in her breast,
And on her lips and o'er her eyes
Spread smiles like light!
(ll. 463–69)

Finally, it is in the name of her mother that Christabel begs Sir Leoline to send away Geraldine, her seducer and oppressor:

'By my mother's soul do I entreat
That thou this woman send away!'
(ll. 616–17)

Christabel's bond with her mother is obviously a source of life within her that sets her apart from others in this world of death. As John Beer says, "Christabel and her dead mother are linked by the power of the organic that subsists deep in the primary consciousness, expressing itself most readily in outgoing love."[3] It is because of this power that Christabel is able to pour out her love on Geraldine in what seems to be a moment of need:

'Thou heard'st a low moaning,
And found'st a bright lady, surpassingly fair;

3. *Coleridge's Poetic Intelligence*, p. 188.

And didst bring her home with thee in love and in charity,
To shield her and shelter her from the damp air.'

(ll. 275-78)

It might be said, in fact, that life and love come close to being identified in the poem: where there is love, there is life; where there is hatred or fear, there is death.

But Christabel's sustaining vision of her mother, the "vision blest," is clearly not of her mother alone. First of all, it seems deliberately left ambiguous: "What if her guardian spirit 'twere, / What if she knew her mother near?" All that the vision does reveal unequivocally is an assurance from heaven "that saints will aid if men will call"; the rest we must grasp by suggestion and implication. However, if we read this against the background of Coleridge's belief that the primal love between mother and child is the "first dawning" of the love of God, we may begin to see that Christabel's "vision blest" implies in fact a vision of her mother as an analogue—a symbol in the Coleridgean sense—of divine reality.[4] The vision is not an obviously transcendent one, but rather—because Christabel is still a child—a vision of her mother, who affords her (or indeed any child) her first image of the divine. Beer calls attention to a very illuminating note Coleridge wrote in 1810, which suggests why Christabel in particular has come to identify mother and heaven: "Christabel—My first cries mingled with my Mother's Death-groan / —and she beheld the vision of Glory ere I the earthly Sun— when I first looked up to Heaven, consciously, it was to look up after or for my Mother—&c &c—"[5] Since her mother died when she was born, Christabel cannot come to a knowledge of heavenly love through the gradual revelation of love from her mother's touches and embraces; she must look directly to heaven, where her mother dwells in glory. In Coleridgean terms, she must bypass the *natura naturata* to search out more directly the *natura naturans*.

Because of her unusually direct apprehension of transcendent reality, Christabel— for all her hold on life—conveys at the same time a sense of spirituality, which accounts in some measure for the innocence and purity we associate with her. In this way she embodies what Anthony Harding has called "spiritual wholeness."[6] Thus, too, prayer is associated with Christabel's innocent spirituality: she is in the midnight wood precisely to pray "for the weal of her lover that's far away" (l. 30); she devoutly calls on Geraldine to pray to the Virgin as they cross the castle courtyard (ll. 137-40); even after her seduction by Geraldine, Christabel, "praying always, prays in sleep" (l. 322), and rising from sleep, she prays again "That He, who on the cross did groan, / Might wash away her sins unknown" (ll. 389-90); and finally, faced with her father's infatuation with Geraldine, she "paused awhile, and inly prayed" (l. 614).

It may be useful, too, to add Harding's observation that "for Coleridge the idea of mother love is closely associated with prayer and the ability to pray."[7] A fascinating

---

4. We may recall that, significantly, some of Coleridge's most beautiful reflections on the love of mother and child appear in the Opus Maximum chapter entitled "The Origin of the Idea of God"; see above, Chapter 1, note 46.

5. *CN*, 3:3720; cited by Beer, *Coleridge's Poetic Intelligence*, p. 191.

6. "Mythopoeic Elements in 'Christabel,' " p. 49.

7. Ibid., p. 47.

notebook entry of 1800, outlining a plan for an essay to be called "Pleasures of Religion," illustrates this strikingly: "Introduction My Mother—prayer in the Lap— prayer by the bed side—prayer in the great Hall at evening / Church—Cathedral— / Mother associated with God—"[8] Again we see how the mother is the mediator of the transcendent, so that Christabel's "vision blest" is a vision both of her mother and of divine reality. While Christabel's link with her mother's spirit is the means by which she achieves, or is granted, "spiritual wholeness," the ultimate source of this spirituality is clearly God.

But if Christabel embodies an "existence-in-the-spirit," Harding goes on to show that Geraldine must be seen as "existence-in-the-flesh": "She belongs to a long and dishonorable tradition of succubae and temptresses, including most notably Spenser's Duessa, in whom the double aspect of the flesh—beautiful to view, but subject to corruption and exercising a tyrannical power over the soul—is imaged."[9] Although Christabel is instinctively loving and prayerful, without the close presence of her nurturing and protecting mother she is vulnerable to the deceits and false attractions of the beautiful Geraldine (who of course bears beneath her garments undisclosed ugliness—"A sight to dream of, not to tell!" l. 253). The struggle thus pits against one another two perennially warring aspects of every human being, the flesh and the spirit. As Harding remarks, "The result of this psychomachy is the transformation of unaffected piety, and the holy sleep of a calm soul, to a state of 'self-inquietude.'"[10]

However, the struggle between Christabel and Geraldine is not between two sharply defined figures. There is clear evidence in the poem that Geraldine is herself divided, that she is ambiguous in her intentions. When Christabel prays, "O mother dear! that thou wert here!" (l. 202), Geraldine's initial reply suggests that she is genuinely moved: "I would, said Geraldine, she were!" (l. 203). But at once another feeling asserts itself, very much at odds with her first response of sympathy:

> But soon with altered voice, said she—
> 'Off, wandering mother! Peak and pine!
> I have power to bid thee flee.'
> Alas! what ails poor Geraldine?
> Why stares she with unsettled eye?
> (ll. 204–8)

Again, not long after, as Geraldine approaches Christabel's bed, she seems to undergo an inner struggle:

8. *CN*, 1:750.

9. "Mythopoeic Elements in 'Christabel,'" p. 48.

10. Ibid. Richard Harter Fogle, seeing "Christabel" as an exemplification of Coleridge's ongoing struggle "to synthesize oppositions into organic unity," has suggested long since that "Christabel and Geraldine may be taken as aspects of the same person," whether in terms of Christabel "as the conscious opposed to Geraldine the unconscious mind, the ego or superego to her id," or (in another mythic mode) as representing "the Uranian and the Pandemonian Aphrodite, sacred versus profane love; or, correspondingly, Agape versus Eros, or Apollo versus Dionysus" (*The Idea of Coleridge's Criticism*, pp. 131–32; for the entire discussion, which remains one of the most illuminating readings of the poem, see pp. 130–59).

Yet Geraldine nor speaks nor stirs;
Ah! what a stricken look was hers!
Deep from within she seems half-way
To lift some weight with sick assay,
And eyes the maid and seeks delay.

(ll. 255–59)

Clearly, we cannot simply equate Geraldine with Spenser's wicked Duessa; this is a more complex figure, perhaps itself compounded of ordered and disordered forces or, even better, of "spiritual" and "fleshly" energies.

Perhaps the very fact that Geraldine is not simply evil, but a figure struggling within itself, suggests that these two warring forces, Christabel and Geraldine—the spirit and the flesh—are not meant to be in opposition. They may be not so much struggling against one another as struggling toward union with one another, and the conflict within Geraldine suggests that in Geraldine this integration, through the agency of Christabel's mother, has already begun: Geraldine is not wholly in the power of the flesh; "spirit" already works in her. The two forces must aim at integration; neither can have its genuine fulfillment without the other. The spirit without the flesh has no true place in the temporal, mortal world, and flesh without spirit is selfish and ignoble.

Coleridge clearly aimed at some kind of resolution, and indeed two proposals for resolution are made in the poem. The first is that of Bard Bracy, whose response to his prophetic dream of the struggle between the dove and the serpent is to propose bringing the two forces into harmony by the power of music. His aim is not to destroy but to reconcile:

'And thence I vowed this self-same day
With music strong and saintly song
To wander through the forest bare,
Lest aught unholy loiter there.'

(ll. 560–63)

The other proposal is that of Sir Leoline, the warrior, whose response to Bracy's dream is, first of all, to misinterpret the figures of the dream—making Geraldine the dove instead of Christabel—and then to propose resolving the conflict by destroying one of the struggling figures:

'Sweet maid, Lord Roland's beauteous dove,
With arms more strong than harp or song,
Thy sire and I will crush the snake!'

(ll. 569–71)

If Bracy is the poet figure, Sir Leoline is the practical man of affairs. In Coleridgean terms, Bracy exercises imagination, the reconciling and mediating faculty; Leoline can achieve only the work of fancy, which deals with "fixities and definites," which are of course all he can see in the world of death over which he presides. Bracy has the use of "reason," which can see beyond the appearances of things, to conceive the spiritual idea beyond; Leoline is caught in the world of mere "understanding," the faculty "which judges according to sense." Bracy's benign influence, sadly, is overborne, at least for the moment, by the single-mindedness of Sir Leoline; the subordinate power becomes the ruling power, and death lords it over life, anger and conflict over love.

* * *

We may now be coming close to the reason Coleridge never finished the poem. His own celebrated apologia, given in the year before his death, does not offer much help: "The reason of my not finishing Christabel is not that I don't know how to do it—for I have, as I always had, the whole plan entire from beginning to end in my mind; but I fear I could not carry on with equal success the execution of the idea, an extremely subtle and difficult one."[11] Coleridge's "Conclusion to Part II," however, which does not seem originally to have been part of the poem but first appeared with it in 1816, is considerably more suggestive:

A little child, a limber elf,
Singing, dancing to itself,
A fairy thing with red round cheeks,
That always finds, and never seeks,
Makes such a vision to the sight
As fills a father's eyes with light;
And pleasures flow in so thick and fast
Upon his heart, that he at last
Must needs express his love's excess
With words of unmeant bitterness.
Perhaps 'tis pretty to force together
Thoughts so all unlike each other;
To mutter and mock a broken charm,
To dally with wrong that does no harm.
Perhaps 'tis tender too and pretty
At each wild word to feel within
A sweet recoil of love and pity.
And what, if in a world of sin
(O sorrow and shame should this be true!)
Such giddiness of heart and brain

11. *TT,* p. 471 (6 July 1833). Wordsworth, who would surely have known of it, did not believe Coleridge had a whole plot in his mind from the beginning. Coleridge's nephew, Justice John Taylor Coleridge, reported in 1836 Wordsworth's belief that Coleridge "had no idea how 'Christabelle' was to have been finished, and he did not think my uncle had ever conceived, in his own mind, any definite plan for it; that the poem had been composed while they were in habits of daily intercourse, and almost in his presence, and when there was the most unreserved intercourse between them as to all their literary projects and productions, and he had never heard from him any plan for finishing it. Not that he doubted my uncle's *sincerity* in his subsequent assertions to the contrary; because, he said, schemes of this sort passed rapidly and vividly through his mind, and so impressed him, that he often fancied he had arranged things, which really and upon trial proved to be mere embryos" (Christopher Wordsworth, *Memoirs of William Wordsworth, Poet-Laureate, D.C.L.,* 2:306–7).

Comes seldom save from rage and pain,
So talks as it's most used to do.

(ll. 656–77)[12]

Insufficient attention has been paid, I believe, to the relationship between these lines and the rest of the poem. Indeed, Arthur Nethercot, the most comprehensive commentator on the poem, dismisses them as "little more than an expression of Coleridge's paternal sentiment toward his young son Hartley," arguing that they add "nothing to help solve the mystery which he here left dangling to baffle posterity."[13] On the contrary, I suggest, these lines represent the poet's own response to his poem and convey at least implicitly the impossibility of reconciling the warring forces of the poem—and hence of completing it. For the conflict is not only in the poem, it is also in the poet himself. Even in the face of his own much loved child, he cannot escape the ambiguities of his finite self; he would like to be all-loving (who indeed would not?), but there is a power within him warring against the spirit of love. A poet might try to join these forces into harmony—"Perhaps 'tis pretty to force together / Thoughts so all unlike each other"—but they cannot, it seems, be reconciled. Even more, the poet suspects that this experience is not only his but that of everyone. It is perhaps not only he who lives with this sin; we may all be living in a "world of sin," where such sad conflict is inevitable.

Something of this is suggested by an intriguing letter written to Coleridge in 1827 by W. G. Kirkpatrick, in which he asks about man's innate relationship to the Good that is God, and his longing for that Good: "Is it that . . . by a Desire there-after given to wed us to it [*i.e.* that good], we being made our absolute self divorced from that same good & left to the Worm of that Desire, to that Hunger as of fire, can only in its nature be a Want a Pain & a Rage (?)" Kirkpatrick then adds a significant marginal note: "(comes seldom save from want & pain) The Love rage & the Wrath rage in Christabel at the Conclusion—why is not Christabel finished?"[14] John Beer points to Coleridge's "presupposition that the energies of wrath and the energies of love are in necessary connection" and argues persuasively that "Coleridge's aim was evidently to show that those energies, properly understood, could be seen to be springing from the same source. All such energies were related to the desire which should unite the human being with God, but which, through failure of connection, turns back to ravage it under forms of wrathful destruction."[15] The conclusion affirms, in effect, that what sad experience—both Christabel's and the poet's—has shown is perhaps inevitable in

12. The lines, which are about Coleridge's son Hartley, first appear in a letter to Southey in 1801; *CL,* 2:728. Coleridge goes on to call the lines "a very metaphysical account of Fathers calling their children rogues, rascals, & little varlets" (p. 729).

13. *The Road to Tryermaine,* p. 55. A more recent study by Constance Hunting, "Another Look at the 'Conclusion to Part II' of *Christabel,*" traces the continuity of words and images between the conclusion and the rest of the poem but fails to offer a convincing thematic connection.

14. MS letter of 12 November 1827 in the Victoria University Library, quoted by Beer, *Coleridge's Poetic Intelligence,* p. 236. Beer conjectures that Kirkpatrick "had evidently either heard Coleridge expounding *Christabel* directly, or seen the relevance of his more general ideas at the end of Part Two."

15. *Coleridge's Poetic Intelligence,* p. 236.

"a world of sin": flesh wars against spirit, selfishness against love. "Christabel" is thus a Coleridgean analogue of the Pauline "war of the members": "The good that I would I do not: but the evil which I would not, that I do. . . . I see another law in my members, warring against the law of my mind, and bringing me into captivity to the law of sin which is in my members" (Rom. 7:19, 23). Christabel has become an unwilling slave of Geraldine, who is her "fleshly self" divorced from spirit. The two aspects of herself that should be in fruitful harmony are in conflict. There is (in Beer's phrase) a "failure of connection."

Clearly, this "failure of connection" between Christabel and Geraldine has its analogues throughout the poem, for there is no relationship in the poem that is fulfilled. Marriage is no more, since Leoline's wife has died, leaving him with only the bells of perpetual mourning. Friendship has been ruptured, for Leoline and Lord Roland de Vaux have become enemies, and even the fresh hope of reconciliation between them is founded on Leoline's dubious relationship with the duplicitous Geraldine; while the newly formed friendship between Christabel and Geraldine has already been betrayed. Romantic love, too, seems to have lost its power, as Christabel longs fruitlessly for her absent lover. Filial love is tenuous at best: the rift between Christabel and her father seems to be of long standing and shows no hope of being bridged, while her relationship with her dead mother—the only one in the poem that is even potentially healthy and life-giving—has not had the support of earthly nurturing and embraces. Finally even divine love, of God for mankind or of mankind for God, remains for Christabel more a longing than an experience of fulfillment. The poem is, in short, a whole world of unfulfilled love—love either failed, or frustrated, or at best ambiguous.

From one point of view—that is, from Coleridge's vantage point that sees maternal love as the origin and grounding of every other love—perhaps Christabel's lack of that earthly mother-love that is manifested in the mother's gaze and the mother's embraces (and of which Coleridge himself felt sadly deprived) placed in jeopardy all the other loves in her world. From another point of view, the issue could be posed in terms of the struggle we have discussed between the flesh and the spirit. If this conflict between aspects of the self that should be acting in harmony is in fact the common state of things in this "world of sin," then there seems little hope not only for Christabel and her lover, or for Christabel and Sir Leoline, but little hope for the fulfillment of any love relationship at all in such a world. In a world where even a loving father speaks "words of unmeant bitterness" to his child, who can escape "rage and pain"?

It may be instructive to recall that the lines that make up the conclusion to "Christabel" were written less than a year before that extraordinary document, Coleridge's verse "Letter to Sara Hutchinson" (4 April 1802). The problem posed in that remarkable outpouring of grief seems much the same: marriage has become "my coarse domestic Life," a clashing of "two discordant Wills"; romantic love, the center of the poem and of his grief, is hopelessly frustrated; the love of his friends, because of their association with his beloved, now "weighs down the Heart"; and even the love of his children has become a joy mingled with regret, so that he has "half-wish'd they never had been born!" If Coleridge did indeed see as early as 1801 the implications of his lines on his child Hartley for his great fragment "Christabel," itself written only a short time earlier, it is fascinating to conjecture that these two so different poems—both in fact incomplete—may have been written out of the same anguish, the same "rage and pain," and that they both portray the same "world of sin."

We shall take up in the next chapter the fate of the "Letter to Sara" and how it was transformed into a poem of incomparable beauty, but as to "Christabel" we are left to conjecture. I have suggested that, in the fragment as we have it—especially in light of the eloquent lines of the poet about his own child—we are shown "a world of sin," in which flesh wars against spirit, death against life; where love is betrayed by duplicity, anger, and pain; where relationships die or fail or turn to conflict. If Coleridge does indeed mean to indict, as the conclusion suggests, not merely himself and Sir Leoline and Geraldine but also the human condition as it exists in this "world of sin," then it is difficult to see how he could have completed the poem. For it may be that what the haunting "Conclusion to Part II" affirms in effect is that the poem is not merely an unfinished story, but the story of our broken and unfinished human life, in which we may at moments—like Christabel—catch a glimpse of the divine "principle of Love," but seek in vain for "objects of a kindred Love" in "fellow-natures." For this is a poem in which the power of love fails, as it did so often for Coleridge in his troubled life.

It tells another tale, with sounds less deep and loud!
A tale of less affright,
And tempered with delight.

— "Dejection: An Ode"

CHAPTER 6

"Dejection":

"A Tale of Less Affright"

Poetic origins are often obscure, as witness the genesis of Shakespeare's sonnets or the history of Keats's two Hyperions. Among such mysteries, the relationship between Coleridge's verse "Letter to Sara Hutchinson" (written on 4 April 1802 but first published only in 1937) and his "Dejection: An Ode" (published in the Morning Post, 4 October 1802, Wordsworth's wedding day) has been a matter of considerable discussion and debate.[1] Although it is evident that the one is a drastic revision of the other, it remains unclear what were Coleridge's poetic purposes in making the revision and what was in his mind in publishing it on the wedding day of his friend Wordsworth, which was also the seventh anniversary of his own unfortunate marriage to Sarah Fricker.

A cogent case has been made that "Dejection" has its origin as much in Coleridge's relationship with Wordsworth as in his frustrated love for Sara Hutchinson. The first four stanzas of Wordsworth's "Immortality Ode," in which Wordsworth laments his loss of the "visionary gleam," were written just days before Coleridge composed his verse letter to Sara, and it was two years before Wordsworth was able to complete his poem. Written as they are on what appears to be a similar theme, it is difficult not to see the two poems as "in some sense in a dialogue with each other."[2] The sense of "dialogue" is deepened when one realizes that Wordsworth's own stanzas echo a poem by Coleridge written two years earlier—"The Mad Monk" (1800), which begins:

> There was a time when earth, and sea, and skies,
>> The bright green vale, and forest's dark recess,
> With all things, lay before mine eyes
>> In steady loveliness:
> But now . . .

(ll. 9–13)

Wordsworth's answer to his sense of loss, written two years after he had begun the

---

1. The text of the "Letter to Sara Hutchinson" used throughout will be that of *CL,* 2:790–98; it may also be found in *Poems,* ed. John Beer, pp. 272–80. I have given line numbers to the text in *CL.* The text of "Dejection: An Ode" is that of *PW,* 1:362–68.

2. George Watson, *Coleridge the Poet,* p. 78. See also Fred Manning Smith, "The Relation of Coleridge's *Ode on Dejection* to Wordsworth's *Ode on Intimations of Immortality.*"

poem, was a reaffirmation of the strength still to be found in the world of nature: "Yet in my heart of hearts I feel your might."³ Coleridge's answer to his loss, it has been said, was rather to turn inward, despairing of nature as a healing power: "O Lady! we receive but what we give" (l. 47). If this is so, the two friends had certainly parted company poetically and philosophically long before their friendship was ruptured in 1810.

Perhaps even more tantalizing is the question of the relationship between the two major versions of Coleridge's poem, the verse letter and the *textus receptus.* As to the poetic superiority of one over the other, each version has its proponents. As Reeve Parker notes, the letter to Sara "has been called an incomparably greater poem . . . chiefly on grounds of its being a less disguised personal lament over marital unhappiness, ill-health, and weakened poetic power." There are others, however, "who prefer the final, shorter ode form for its greater lyric dignity and who find the sprawling earlier text embarrassing in its self-pity."⁴

John Beer, for example, seems to give the nod to the earlier version: "Both poems have their peculiar value. *Dejection* stands to its predecessor rather as an engraving may stand in relation to an original painting. Its points are made more sharply and stringently: but in order to hear the full throb of Coleridge's unhappiness the greater length of the earlier version is needed."⁵ Humphry House, too, although he admits that a "case cannot be made out for the full coherence of the original version," argues for its overall superiority, stressing what he sees as its greater artistic unity; he argues, in effect, that "Dejection" betrays the essential unity of the original.⁶ George Watson, on the other hand, insists: "There can be no doubt of the superiority of the final version, where the original 340 lines have been reduced to a tight-packed 139. . . . On the whole, . . . the reduction of the ode to its familiar form is a continuous triumph of critical acumen."⁷ In the last analysis, it comes down no doubt to a matter of poetic taste, a conflict (as Reeve Parker characterizes it) "between those who like confessional sincerity in art and those whose inclination is for the orderliness of form."⁸

We are faced, however, with the two major versions of the poem; and one question that seems continually to be urged in the recent history of Coleridge criticism is Coleridge's purpose in changing the form of the poem so drastically. Some critics have suggested that Coleridge found it necessary, for personal reasons, to hide (or suppress) the real origins of his feelings; others, that he realized his real theme was the loss of his "shaping spirit of Imagination," and so pruned and reshaped the poem to highlight that loss; and still others, that, having experienced such deep grief, he used "Dejec-

---

3. "Ode: Intimations of Immortality," l. 190, in *The Poetical Works of William Wordsworth,* ed. Ernest de Selincourt and Helen Darbishire, 4:279.
4. *Coleridge's Meditative Art,* p. 180.
5. *Poems,* ed. Beer, p. 257.
6. *Coleridge: The Clark Lectures 1951–52,* p. 137; see also pp. 133–37.
7. *Coleridge the Poet,* pp. 74–75.
8. *Coleridge's Meditative Art,* p. 180. A different focus of this distinction is given by Max F. Schulz in his bibliographical essay "Coleridge": "It is probably safe to say that those interested in Coleridge the man and in the biographical facts behind the composition of the poem will prefer the 'Verse Letter,' while those concerned with literary questions of theme and form will be drawn to 'Dejection'" (p. 203).

tion" to explore the process of grief with which the experience began. Each of these approaches has something to recommend it, nor should they be thought of as necessarily exclusive of one another.

The first of these views—that Coleridge found it necessary to suppress the real origins of his feelings—may be represented by Beverly Fields's interesting psychoanalytic study, *Reality's Dark Dream*. Her case can be fairly enough summed up in these words from her conclusion: "The shifts in organization appear to have been made partly for reasons of coherence but also partly in order to suppress as far as possible the real reasons for his depression. It was undoubtedly far easier for him to assign the cause of the depression to metaphysical speculation than it would have been to let the poem stand as a revelation of the sadomasochistic fantasies that paralyzed his feeling and his behavior."[9] Other, less psychoanalytic readers, like Max Schulz and Charles Bouslog, also see Coleridge's desire to camouflage his real feelings as the reason for his revision of the poem.[10]

The second reading—that Coleridge realized his real theme was the loss of his "shaping spirit of Imagination"—is persuasively argued by Paul Magnuson in *Coleridge's Nightmare Poetry*. Magnuson finds, in effect, not two versions of the same poem but two quite distinct poems. The "Letter" focuses on "the pain he has caused Asra," while "Dejection" focuses on himself—his own pain, his own loss. "The Letter is nearer the spirit of the earlier Conversation Poems in that there is an imagined exchange of sympathy, but in 'Dejection,' he faces a far more fundamental problem. If he himself has lost joy, and if he is the victim of strong feelings, then his blessing could well turn into a curse upon himself and Asra."[11] He has lost, perhaps forever, his old sense of the One Life. As Magnuson puts it, "We project a meaning upon nature, and whatever we receive from nature is only a reflection of our minds,"[12] but since the poet has lost joy and his "shaping spirit of Imagination" (l. 86), for him the world is now without meaning. There is still hope for "the Lady," since her soul is still alive—and so for her all things can still live, "their life the eddying of her living soul!" (l. 136)—but for him there is no life in the world because there is no life within him: "O Lady! we receive but what we give."

The third view—that Coleridge, having experienced such deep grief, used "Dejection" to explore the process of grief itself—is beautifully articulated by Reeve Parker in *Coleridge's Meditative Art*. The ode was, in effect, a gesture "offered to reassure the Grasmere circle that he was capable of transcending the impulses toward despair and unseemliness that were so much responsible for the original letter."[13] The original letter is merely an expression of grief, while the more shapely, more carefully crafted ode is an exploration of the state of grief in which the poet finds himself. This exploration is, in effect and even perhaps in intention, a kind of therapy. As Coleridge had

9. *Reality's Dark Dream: Dejection in Coleridge*, p. 166; see also pp. 101–64.

10. See Schulz, *The Poetic Voices of Coleridge*, p. 140; and Bouslog, "Structure and Theme in Coleridge's 'Dejection: An Ode.'"

11. *Coleridge's Nightmare Poetry*, pp. 108, 109; for Magnuson's complete reading of the poems, see pp. 107–25.

12. Ibid., p. 114.

13. *Coleridge's Meditative Art*, p. 181; for Parker's full interpretation, see pp. 180–209.

argued in the preface to his *Poems* of 1796, from the intellectual labor of poetic composition "a pleasure results which is gradually associated and mingles as a corrective with the painful subject of the description."[14] Thus there is, in Parker's phrase, "a salutary egotism in poetic composition."[15]

Parker thus finds "Dejection" a much more positive poetic experience than do many other critics. He believes, in fact, that modern readers of the poem often read into it their own preoccupations: "In emphasizing the elements of personal distress discernible in and through the poem and in seeing it as a lament over suspended poetic imagination, readers . . . have presumed a greater continuity than actually exists between the concerns of a poet like Coleridge, at the turn of the nineteenth century, and the characteristic preoccupation of many twentieth-century writers with alienation, self-doubt, and distrust of the artful imagination."[16]

There is an entry from 1803 in one of Coleridge's notebooks that Parker believes sheds light on Coleridge's "heuristic" motives in "Dejection": "One excellent use of communication of Sorrows to a Friend is this: that in relating what ails us we ourselves first know exactly what the real Grief is—& see it for itself, in its own form and limits."[17] With the help of the controlling metaphor of the poem, the storm, the poet is able to dramatize his situation—and, in doing so, is able to "generalize" his grief, to (in a phrase of Coleridge) abstract "the thoughts and images from their original cause" and to reflect on them "with less and less reference to the individual suffering that had been their first subject."[18] When the poet returns, late in the poem, to an awareness of the wind that still rages, he is able to achieve, in Parker's phrase, an "absolute distancing of wind and poet."[19] He is not under the control of the wind but rather can hear in it different voices, as he soon reveals—hearing first the voices of violence and war, then a new voice, "A tale of less affright, / And tempered with delight" (ll. 118–19). He can now hear in the wind the voice of Wordsworth's Lucy Gray, and it is a voice of life even within the sound of the lonesome wind.

For Parker, then, the "sounds less deep and loud" at the end of stanza VII are "correlative to a mind that, having gone through the process of deliberately exploring the melancholy grief with which the poem opens, is winning its way to a substantial calm." Having achieved this calm, the poet is then able "to 'send his soul abroad' in the blessing that constitutes the final stanza."[20]

Without in any way denying the cogency of Parker's approach, with which I find myself generally in considerable agreement, I would like to go on to suggest that there is a motif implicit in "Dejection" that is quite compatible with the exploration of the process of grief—a motif that has been given little or no attention.

* * *

14. *PW,* 2:1136; quoted by Parker, *Coleridge's Meditative Art,* pp. 181–82.

15. *Coleridge's Meditative Art,* p. 181.

16. Ibid.

17. *CN,* 1:1599; quoted by Parker, *Coleridge's Meditative Art,* p. 182.

18. From one of two letters Coleridge contributed to *Blackwood's Magazine* in 1821 on the uses of meditation; in *Notes and Lectures upon Shakespeare . . . with Other Literary Remains,* ed. Mrs. H. N. Coleridge, in *Complete Works,* ed. W. G. T. Shedd, 4:435. See also Parker, *Coleridge's Meditative Art,* p. 193.

19. Parker, *Coleridge's Meditative Art,* p. 200.

20. Ibid., pp. 206–7.

Let me begin with the "Letter to Sara." No one would deny, I suspect, that the letter, whatever else it is about—loss or grief or despair—is also about love. It may be love lost or grieved over or despaired of, but any careful reading makes it clear how preoccupied the original poem is with love. And this love ranges through the whole spectrum of possibilities. The most obvious—and indeed central—love is what we may call his "romantic" love for Sara Hutchinson. She is his "best belov'd! who lovest me the best" (l. 120); she is "My Comforter! A Heart within my Heart!" (l. 250); she is the "Sister & Friend of my devoutest Choice!" (l. 324). She is beyond question the central figure of the letter addressed to her. At the same time, however, the context in which she is placed must be taken account of: she is constantly seen as part of a whole domestic scene, as in "that happy night / When Mary, thou & I together were, / The low decaying Fire our only Light" (ll. 99–101), or when he speaks despairingly of visiting "those, I love, as I love thee, / Mary, & William, & dear Dorothy" (ll. 157–58). Not only Sara but also the loving circle of which she is part is the object of his love and longing. This is not to say that there is no romantic or sexual component in his longing for Sara; there clearly is. It is to suggest, however, that there is more than one kind of love at issue, not only in the poem but even in his relationship with Sara.

With this peacefully remembered scene of domestic tranquillity, Coleridge contrasts his own home: "My own peculiar Lot, my house-hold Life / It is, & will remain, Indifference or Strife" (ll. 163–64). It is, perhaps even more movingly, "my coarse domestic life" (l. 258). There is joy, to be sure, in the love of his children: "My Little Children are a Joy, a Love, / A good Gift from above!" (ll. 272–73). But his grief (perhaps over the failure of his own domestic life) lessens the joy of even this great love: "This clinging Grief too, in it's turn, awakes / That Love, and Father's Joy; but O! it makes / The Love the greater, & the Joy far less" (ll. 287–89).

There is love of Nature in the poem, too, for he goes on to extol its beauty:

> These Mountains too, these Vales, these Woods, these Lakes,
> Scenes full of Beauty & of Loftiness
> Where all my Life I fondly hop'd to live—
> I were sunk low indeed, did they *no* solace give.
>
> (ll. 290–93)

But even they have failed him, for—and here the Wordsworthian parallel will be evident—"They are not to me the Things, which once they were" (l. 295).

Thus there is in the "Letter to Sara" a whole range of human loves: romantic and sexual love, love of family, love of children, love of friends, love of nature.[21] All are

21. This spectrum of loves in the "Letter to Sara" may account, in some measure, for the different addressees of its various versions: the very personal "Sara" of the original; "William," "Wordsworth," and "dearest poet" (in the version Coleridge sent to William Sotheby in a letter of 19 July 1802; *CL*, 2:813–19), emphasizing his close personal relationship with his poet-friend; "Edmund" (in the version published in the *Morning Post* on 4 October 1802; see *PW*, 1:362–68, notes), again celebrating friendship, though distanced by the use of another name; and "Lady" (in the *textus receptus* published in *Sibylline Leaves* in 1816), returning to the romantic love of the original verse letter, but again distanced by the use of the generic and more formal mode of address. Coleridge's complex thought and feeling give validity to each of these in turn.

either lessened or lost or in some way frustrated. One may well say that the "Letter" is about loss, but I suggest that even more fundamental to it is the question of what it is that is lost: love of every kind. The most basic dichotomy of the "Letter" is between Coleridge and Sara—the one who has lost love and the one who is still surrounded by it, as the last stanza continues to insist:

> Sister & Friend of my devoutest Choice!
> Thou being innocent & full of love,
> And nested with the Darlings of thy Love . . .
>   (ll. 324–26)

Whatever else it is, the "Letter to Sara" is a poem about love and its loss.

Against this background, it is perhaps startling to discover that while the word *love* (or its cognates *loved, lover,* and *beloved*) appears twenty-one times in the "Letter," its only cognate in "Dejection" is, ironically, "loveless" in line 52. Does this mean that a motif that was so prominent in the earlier version has been completely written out of the later one?

Although he is not directly addressing this question (the total disappearance of the word *love* in "Dejection" seems not to have been noticed before), George Dekker does suggest that the change of focus, from the preoccupation with the failure of love in the "Letter" to an emphasis on the poet's loss of the "shaping spirit of Imagination," is caused by a change of view in Coleridge concerning the relative importance of various influences in his life. Coleridge had suffered a prolonged illness during the winter of 1800–1801, during which he experienced considerable physical pain; he took refuge from his pain not only in opium (this seems to have been the real beginning of his addiction) but also in "abstruse research." Dekker argues that "Coleridge emerged from that terrible winter with a greater need than ever for unqualified sympathy and reassurance—which Sara Fricker had been unable to provide in the best of times." He also emerged, Dekker goes on, "with a need to explain and perhaps even excuse a collapse which—in actuality and in the account given in the ode—had something mysterious and self-engendered about it."[22] In the verse letter, Coleridge was "telling Sara Hutchinson and himself that his ill-starred marriage was at the bottom of it all: of his loss of Joy, of his 'abstruse research' and therefore of his loss of the shaping spirit of Imagination." In the ensuing months, however, Coleridge seems to have had "second thoughts" about what had driven him to the loss of his "shaping spirit," attributing it to his "long & exceedingly severe Metaphysical Investigations" (as he wrote to Southey), and only secondarily to ill health and "private afflictions." What had changed, Dekker concludes, was that in editing the "Letter" for publication in the *Morning Post* for 4 October 1802, he was writing in a "more honest and forgiving spirit."[23]

This is an ingenious and tantalizing conjecture—and indeed a useful one, in that it highlights Coleridge's movement toward a more balanced view of his troubles: it is not merely "blighted affection" that has brought him to this sad pass. He has come to

22. *Coleridge and the Literature of Sensibility,* p. 41.
23. Ibid., pp. 41–42, 43.

recognize that the reality is considerably more complex than he had realized—both the reality of his life and the reality of his love relationships. However, I cannot find ultimately convincing Dekker's argument that the focus of the poem has changed from love to the loss of imagination. The total deletion of a word that had appeared, in one form or another, no less than twenty-one times in the earlier version cannot be without significance, especially since its only vestige is the haunting word *loveless*. The omission suggests too strongly that the poet was not merely shifting focus or changing emphasis but revealing either a deliberate or unconscious "avoidance mechanism." Whether conscious or unconscious, the omission of the word is of telling significance. I shall argue, in fact, that the word *loveless*—"the poor loveless ever-anxious crowd"— is a key to the poem. Love, far from being replaced by imagination as the focal point of the poem, becomes—through the agency of the poet's ironic meditation on joy and through the power of nature—more intensely linked with imagination, both as theme and as operative principle of the poem. The love that was explicit throughout the "Letter" becomes more subtly pervasive, as an implicit principle of action in "Dejection."

My argument turns around the interpretation of the much-quoted line "O Lady! we receive but what we give" (l. 47). This line is most commonly taken to refer to the poet's relationship with nature: to mean that he is arguing, in effect, against Wordsworth's belief in the healing power of nature. Nature has no power to affect our lives; our response to nature is determined by our own feelings, by the projection of our selves. If our feelings, or our inner selves, have lost their sense of life, then there is nothing but the blankness of despair.

This may indeed be the initial meaning of the line, but it does not, I think, remain its sole meaning. This understanding of the relationship of nature and self does last, to be sure, through the two stanzas that follow—stanza V, which extols joy, "this strong music in the soul" (l. 60), and stanza VI, which laments the passing of that joy. Stanza VII, however, marks a decisive turn away from this view:

> Hence, viper thoughts, that coil around my mind,
>   Reality's dark dream!
> I turn from you, and listen to the wind,
>   Which long has raved unnoticed.
>
>   (ll. 94–97)

Putting aside the almost solipsistic view of himself and nature, he finally allows himself really to listen to the wind, to allow *its* power to work in him. At the beginning of the poem, he had projected his own feelings onto the wind—and so could hear only his own depression. This is precisely what had led to his reflection: "We receive but what we give." Later, after rejecting this self-centered and self-pitying attitude ("Hence, viper thoughts!"), he is able to let nature touch him, and he finds that it is healing. Perhaps Wordsworth is right after all.[24]

---

24. An opposite view of the wind metaphor is taken by Panthea Reid Broughton in her subtle and perceptive essay "The Modifying Metaphor in 'Dejection: An Ode'": "Coleridge was really very skep-

Therefore stanza IV was a self-pitying, wrongheaded view, which the poet now finds strength to reject; and the vehicle for this discovery is the wind. His perception of the wind had begun as superstition (the folk beliefs concerning the weather) and self-projection; but through the process of the poem he has come to see it as a natural force from which he can learn: it has its cycles, from wild to gentle, as does he himself.[25] As the wind gentles down—singing "a tale of less affright, / And tempered with delight"—so does his own soul. Thus he was correct at the end of stanza IV:

> And from the soul itself must there be sent
> A sweet and potent voice, of its own birth,
> Of all sweet sounds the life and element!
> (ll. 56–58)

This is the voice that issues forth from him at the end of the poem, offering blessing to one he loves. It is perhaps no accident that in stanza IV this voice is contrasted with "the poor loveless ever-anxious crowd"—because we come to see that it is the voice of love, of one who has learned that only if he is open to receive will he be able to give. Had he not opened himself to the voice of nature—first wild but ultimately healing— he would never have found his own voice. But he did find it, and in the closing lines of blessing it is indeed "a sweet and potent voice," newly potent because it now speaks not out of self-pity but out of loving concern for another.

The pattern of this poem is, in fact, not unlike that of a number of other Coleridge poems. It is similar in this regard, for example, to "This Lime-Tree Bower My Prison," in which the poet overcomes his dejection by entering into the feelings of Charles Lamb as he enjoys the country sunset:

> and sometimes
> 'Tis well to be bereft of promis'd good,

---

tical . . . of the Wordsworthian faith in the active universe" (p. 242). Although she later sees Coleridge able to use the closing image of the "eddy" as a fruitful metaphor, in Broughton's view Coleridge begins by "dispelling the familiar Romantic metaphor of the Aeolian harp. . . . Outward forms, though they may rescue Wordsworth, fail Coleridge; he awaits their intervention to no avail. And thus the central Romantic metaphor debilitates because it encourages him to wait passively for a shift in the weather before he can change his tune" (p. 243). I suggest rather that the poet's waiting has changed from passive to active ("I turn from you"), as he opens himself at last to the natural influence of the wind that he had shut out. For a view similar to Broughton's, see Marshall Suther, *The Dark Night of Samuel Taylor Coleridge,* pp. 124–28.

Unlike Broughton, M. H. Abrams, in "The Correspondent Breeze: A Romantic Metaphor," sees the wind as truly an agent for change in the poet's mind: "By the agency of the wind storm it describes, the poem turns out to contradict its own premises: the poet's spirit awakens to violent life even as he laments his inner death" (in *English Romantic Poets: Modern Essays in Criticism,* ed. Abrams, p. 39). Richard Harter Fogle, too, in "The Dejection of Coleridge's Ode," assumes that "Coleridge as a metaphysical realist and a Romantic poet of nature is expressing his experience through the interaction of his thoughts and emotions with natural symbolism and imagery" (p. 73).

25. In "Structure and Style in the Greater Romantic Lyric," M. H. Abrams notes: "On Coleridge's philosophical premises, in this poem nature is made thought and thought nature, both by their sustained interaction and by their seamless metaphoric continuity" (in *Romanticism and Consciousness: Essays in Criticism,* ed. Harold Bloom, p. 223).

That we may lift the soul, and contemplate
With lively joy the joys we cannot share.
                    (ll. 64–67)

What is this but an act of love: a giving of oneself to another. And so with the Ancient Mariner, who is able to move out of his isolation by an act of imaginative sympathy with the water snakes:

A spring of love gushed from my heart,
And I blessed them unaware.
                    (ll. 284–85)

Whatever name one may give to such an act, it is a movement of love: a going forth out of the self to encounter the being of another. In the last analysis, Coleridge is not content to remain one of the "loveless ever-anxious crowd"; he does not remain mired in "dejection." Through the ministry of nature, he is able to love. "Dejection" remains, therefore, in its transformation from the "Letter to Sara," a love poem; but it becomes a love poem in a broader and deeper sense—not merely the lament of a frustrated lover but an ode to the power of love itself, which can bring him out of dejection into calm, out of selfishness and self-pity into generous-hearted blessing.

*   *   *

But if "Dejection" is about love, it is also about imagination and joy—for the three are inextricably bound together—and about the power of art. That "Dejection" is concerned with imagination is perhaps the best known truth about the poem: the poet is dejected at least in part because he has lost his "shaping spirit of Imagination" (l. 86). He has allowed the understanding—the analytic faculty, the power of mind that deals with parts and with merely sense impressions—to take away his power to shape his experience of the world into a meaningful whole: "by abstruse research to steal / From my own nature all the natural man" (ll. 89–90).

What is it, though, that has brought him to this sad pass? Surely it is the loss of joy, the very joy that he wishes for the "virtuous Lady." For joy is

the spirit and the power,
Which wedding Nature to us gives in dower
A new Earth and new Heaven.
                    (ll. 67–69)[26]

26. Attention has been called to the echo here of Revelation 21:1 ("And I saw a new heaven and a new earth"), but I have not seen reference to the possibly even deeper roots of this passage in Isaiah 65:17ff., where the role of joy is made explicit: "For, behold, I create new heavens and a new earth: and the former shall not be remembered, nor come into mind. But be ye glad and rejoice for ever in that which I create: for, behold, I create Jerusalem a rejoicing, and her people a joy. And I will rejoice in Jerusalem, and joy in my people: and the voice of weeping shall be no more heard in her, nor the voice of crying." With the notes struck not only of joy but also of creativity, together with the fact that in Revelation Jerusalem becomes the Bride, it is difficult not to hear echoes of both passages in Coleridge's lines.

As we saw earlier, joy is the effect of love: the ecstasy of communion with "the other," in which love, given and received, becomes a celebration of shared being and good-ness. It is joy that can enable one to bring together man and nature, heaven and earth, sense experience and spiritual reality, and it is at the same time joy that celebrates the union of all these things. The "natural man" could feel joy, for he was in harmony with nature and could not only perceive but also feel the unity of all creation. His faculties all in harmony, he could appreciate the "wholeness" of experience and rejoice in it, for wholeness and joy are functions of one another. Hence the joyful exclamation of "The Eolian Harp": "O! the one Life within us and abroad" (l. 26). However, having "by abstruse research" narrowed down his vision of the world, the poet can now see only parts of the great world. And with the loss of wholeness, joy is lost.

For joy is not only a feeling but also a power of perception; it affords both creative vision and emotional exaltation. Joy or "delight" is, in fact, a prerequisite not only for harmonious living but also for the writing of poetry. As Coleridge had written of the Abyssinian maid:

> Could I revive within me
> Her symphony and song,
> To such a deep delight 'twould win me,
> That with music loud and long,
> I would build that dome in air . . .
> ("Kubla Khan," ll. 42–46)

This is, I suggest, precisely the role of "Lucy Gray," the tale "tempered with delight." The poet has revived within himself, or the wind has raised within him, or better yet, the poet and the wind in fruitful concert have revived, a song—not the song of the Abyssinian maid but the song sung by the little girl. As Irene Chayes says, "The poet of 'Dejection' begins in his reverie to re-compose another man's poem and for the moment becomes a poet again."[27] His imagination has come to life again.

The imagination is, for Coleridge, a cognitive power of a very high order. Up to this point in the poem, the poet has still been limited to the knowledge given by the understanding ("abstruse research"). Coleridge wrote some years later of the discur-sive understanding that its characteristic is "Clearness without Depth. It contemplates the unity of things in their *limits* only, and is consequently a knowledge of superficies without substance." Limited to the power of the understanding, the poet can describe completely and accurately the things that surround him—the "New-moon winter-bright," the yellow green tint of the western sky, the "thin clouds above"—but he can know only their surfaces, their "limits": "I see them all so excellently fair, / I see, not feel, how beautiful they are!" Far above this limited power, however, is "the complet-ing power which unites clearness with depth, the plenitude of the sense with the comprehensibility of the understanding," that is, "the IMAGINATION, impregnated with which the understanding itself becomes intuitive, and a living power."[28]

27. "Rhetoric as Drama: An Approach to the Romantic Ode," p. 70.
28. *LS,* p. 69.

The imagination is, too, the synthetic power, by which things are brought into order and relation. How inclusive Coleridge intends this synthetic power to be can be seen most clearly in the classic formulation in chapter 14 of the *Biographia Literaria:*

> The poet, described in *ideal* perfection, brings the whole soul of man into activity, with the subordination of its faculties to each other, according to their relative worth and dignity. He diffuses a tone, and spirit of unity, that blends, and (as it were) *fuses,* each into each, by that synthetic and magical power, to which we have exclusively appropriated the name of imagination. This power, first put in action by the will and understanding, and retained under their irremissive, though gentle and unnoticed, controul *(laxis effertur habenis)* reveals itself in the balance or reconciliation of opposite or discordant qualities: of sameness, with difference; of the general, with the concrete; the idea, with the image; the individual, with the representative; the sense of novelty and freshness, with old and familiar objects; a more than usual state of emotion, with more than usual order; judgment ever awake and steady self-possession, with enthusiasm and feeling profound or vehement; and while it blends and harmonizes the natural and the artificial, still subordinates art to nature; the manner to the matter; and our admiration of the poet to our sympathy with the poetry.[29]

Through such a faculty the individual human experience can be perceived not in isolation—as the poet has been doing in stanzas I-VI of "Dejection"—but in relation to the larger reality of the world, including the human community, for, as it brings "the whole soul of man into activity," it embraces not only the concrete but also the general, the representative together with the individual, at the same time that it breaks through the mere surface knowledge afforded by the understanding to "a more than usual state of emotion, with more than usual order." Here is precisely what the dejected poet, turned in upon himself, needs to liberate his shackled spirit: his "shaping spirit of Imagination."

But let us return to the role of joy. How can a tale that tells of the suffering of a frightened child—her moans and grief and fear—be a cause of "delight" for the poet, or indeed for anyone? The answer has to do with the nature of aesthetic experience. The wind is, after all, a "Poet, e'en to frenzy bold" (l. 109). Through the agency of the wind and the power of the poet's poet-friend—his synthesizing power of imagination—the actual experience of grief (both Coleridge's grief and the grief of the lost child) is transformed into a tale, an artistic form, that distances the listener from the actual experience, giving it shape and meaning and universal significance. The terrifying experience is thus sublimated to another level of reality, a mythic level, that is both meaningful and sustaining. For myth—the product of imagination, which brings together in a single vision "the general, with the concrete," "the individual, with the representative"—universalizes our experiences, showing them to be part of the larger experience of mankind; by binding us to each other through our common humanity, especially through our common experience of suffering, myth allows us to draw strength from each other. It is thus we learn that mankind survives even in the face of diminishment and loss. Therefore the experience the poet could not bear becomes through a work of imagination (the "tale" that the wind tells) not only bearable but even hopeful.

29. *BL,* 2:15–17.

This is not to say, of course, that the grief is taken away in the "tale." It retains, for the reader as well as for the poet, a strong sense of the terror of the child irretrievably lost. The terror is, however, "tempered" by art, so that the grief is bearable and life can go on. If the tale of the wind has made the child's grief bearable to the hearer, so the poet's tale of his own grief (his poem, "Dejection") may serve the same function, giving him enough "distance" from his grief that he can bear it—and that life can go on.

Rachel Trickett has remarked that the secret of morality in Wordsworth is that love must precede understanding.[30] Her comment recalls Shelley's famous dictum in the "Defence of Poetry" that "the great secret of morals is love, or a going out of our own nature and an identification of ourselves with the beautiful which exists in thought, action, or person, not our own."[31] What Trickett, like Shelley, has in mind of course is not merely morality but poetry, as a distillation and articulation of the highest human values. If this is true of Wordsworth, it is no less true of Coleridge; without love there can be no poetry. Without love, no joy; without joy, no working of that shaping power, imagination.

But since the three—love, joy, and imagination—work so closely in concert, any one of them can help to rouse the others. In "Dejection," the momentary return of imagination and imaginative delight—in the poet's recollection of "Lucy Gray"—can stir in him a return of love, moving him to the loving gesture of blessing that closes the poem, and can hold out at least the hope of a more personal joy for him, as he prays for the gift of joy for one he loves.

* * *

One question remains: what did Coleridge mean by publishing "Dejection" on Wordsworth's wedding day and his own anniversary? I would like to suggest that he intended the poem as a kind of ironic epithalamion, for himself rather than for his friend. For Coleridge's tribute to the power of love is bound up, however subtly, with the nuptial imagery of the first half of the poem. The nuptial portrayed is, of course, the marriage between Nature and man, and joy presides over the solemnity:

Joy, Lady! is the spirit and the power,
Which wedding Nature to us gives in dower
A new Earth and new Heaven.
(ll. 67–69)

But this wedding involves, paradoxically, both life and death:

And in our life alone does Nature live:
Ours is her wedding garment, ours her shroud.
(ll. 48–49)

30. "Wordsworth's Moral Imagination," lecture delivered at the Wordsworth Summer Conference, Grasmere, 3 August 1983.
31. Percy Bysshe Shelley, "A Defence of Poetry," in *Shelley's Prose,* ed. David Lee Clark, pp. 282–83.

Yet, if our union with Nature implies death, it does so in a sense analogous to sexual union as "a little death"—a death that can bring about new life, in this case indeed "a new Earth and new Heaven." So too the "phantom light" (l. 11)—the ghost of the old moon held in the arms of the new—implies death, while the new moon affirms life. The old moon must die if the new moon is to be born. (One might even suggest that the "silver thread" with which the phantom light is "rimmed and circled" might point ahead to the "wedding garment.") Thus the phases of the moon, which are of course cycles of Nature, are caught up in the nuptial imagery, which itself, as Robert Siegel has suggested, "reflects the theme of imaginative wholeness."[32]

However, in striking contrast to the ideal marriage described in stanza V, in which Joy, "wedding Nature to us gives in dower / A new Earth and new Heaven," there is the poet's own wedding with Nature (stanza VII), which brings forth not "a new Earth and new Heaven" but a terrifying storm. The storm is not to last forever, though, for the poet hears at length another voice of Nature:

> A tale of less affright,
> And tempered with delight.
>> (ll. 118–19)

If the poet's stormy wedding with Nature—which is indeed more like a divorce than a marriage—may be seen as metaphor for Coleridge's ill-fated marriage to Sarah Fricker, then the incomplete but longed-for union with the kinder face of Nature ("tempered with delight") may be taken as a metaphor for his impossible yet somehow sustaining union with Sara Hutchinson.

Coleridge's marriage to Sarah Fricker is over, no doubt, leaving behind only a "phantom light" like that of the old moon, and marriage to Sara Hutchinson is only a longing. But if the song the poet hears in the wind is indeed "Lucy Gray," then there is at least a sustaining dream at the end. Lucy Gray is dead, to be sure, but she is still alive as a dream, a mythic reality, as Lucy "sings a solitary song / That whistles in the wind." So too the poet's love for "the other Sara" is alive for him, at least as a comforting dream.

But this love is not merely a dream; like the song sung by Lucy Gray, it has something of the healing power of myth. As Coleridge's spiritual divorce from his wife is reflected in his divorce from Nature, from "the one Life within us and abroad," the "sympathy between his soul and Sara Hutchinson's looks forward to a new wedding of his soul to nature."[33] He too, I might add, like Lucy Gray, sings his "solitary song"— this poem—that "whistles in the wind," affirming life even in the midst of death.

This is indeed the power of love: to bless, to heal, even—and even in the face of dejection—to bring the hope of joy. And the power of love is, as we have seen, for

---

32. "The Serpent and the Dove: The Problem of Evil in Coleridge's Poetry," p. 236. I am more generally grateful to Siegel, too, for his illuminating discussion of the wedding theme, which has considerably influenced my own reading of the poem.
33. Ibid., p. 238.

Coleridge as for Wordsworth, deeply bound up with imaginative power. Wordsworth wrote, at the end of *The Prelude:*

> This spiritual Love acts not nor can exist
> Without Imagination.
>   (14.188–89; 1850 version)

Coleridge would stress, I think, the corollary: that imagination cannot exist without love. He could write this poem only because the love he thought he had lost was not wholly dead in him, because—whether or not his love was returned—he was still, or perhaps again, capable of giving love. Perhaps indeed his gift of love was all the greater because it was at last unconditional love, given not for his sake but for the sake of the beloved, given whether or not it was returned. In that generous-hearted gift of self lay his hope.

There is one significant difference in this poem from the pattern of the conversation poems, with which "Dejection" otherwise has so much in common: here, there is no transforming vision; the power of the *natura naturans* has here eluded the poet. Yet, I suggest, Coleridge—like Wordsworth in the "Intimations Ode"—in the end "grieves not," but "rather finds strength in what remains behind." The *natura naturata,* in the wind and in his beloved friend, still has power to strengthen him. This is a night-poem, after all, which ends at midnight, and whatever light there may be is from the moon. Though the sun may not now shine for him, the poet knows that the moonlight comes from the same source, however dim a reflection it may be. The moon testifies to the ongoing power of the sun—just as the imagined joy of his friend testifies, however dimly, to the source of joy, and therefore to the possibility of joy for him. As it is love that makes possible now this vicarious joy, so it is love that holds out hope of other joy yet to come.

Since all that beat about in Nature's range,
Or veer or vanish; why should'st thou remain
The only constant in a world of change,
O yearning Thought! that liv'st but in the brain?

—*"Constancy to an Ideal Object"*

Unchanged within, to see all changed without,
Is a blank lot and hard to bear, no doubt.
Yet why at others' wanings should'st thou fret?
Then only might'st thou feel a just regret,
Hadst thou withheld thy love or hid thy light
In selfish forethought of neglect and slight.

—*"Duty Surviving Self-Love"*

Yet haply there will come a weary day,
When overtask'd at length
Both Love and Hope beneath the load give way.
Then with a statue's smile, a statue's strength,
Stands the mute sister, Patience, nothing loth,
And both supporting does the work of both.

—*"Love, Hope, and Patience in Education"*

CHAPTER 7

"Constancy" and Other Late Poems:

"Love and Hope Beneath the Load"

Just as in "Dejection" there was no joyful resolution for Coleridge, neither was there in the poetry of the years to come. There were, however, times of hope and even moments of joy, for even in the darkest times there was always love in Coleridge's life.

Until fairly recently, Coleridge's later poetry was given relatively little serious attention. Even as late as twenty years ago, for example, George Watson was able to sum up over thirty years of Coleridge's poetry by saying, "The great theme of the last poems, first fully stated in the Dejection Ode of 1802, is unrequited love."[1] The only poem to which Watson gives more than a passing glance is "The Garden of Boccaccio," which is singled out not as representative of Coleridge's later work but precisely because it is seen as an anachronism, harking back to the earlier style and spirit of the conversation poems.

However, the later poems both deserve and require a more subtle approach than this; both in substance and in style they have a life of their own. Their themes are much broader and deeper than simply "unrequited love," and their styles are many and varied. As John Mahoney has said, Coleridge "continued to write a great variety of poems in a great variety of manners, not only those of black disillusionment that are relatively well known and occasionally anthologized, but also those less well known expressions of joy, however transitory, and those more overtly religious poems of prayer and resignation."[2] Even the most cursory reading of the later work reveals poems as anguished as "Limbo" (1811) or as beautifully visionary as the sonnet "Fancy in Nubibus" (1817), as haunting and nostalgic as "First Advent of Love" (?1824), as good-humoredly indignant as "Lines, to a Comic Author, on an Abusive Review" (?1825), or as charming and serene as that splendid poem "The Garden of Boccaccio" (1828).

Even in terms of the more limited focus of this study—the role of love in Coleridge's poems—one must be careful not to oversimplify, by seeing love as forever lost to him

1. *Coleridge the Poet*, p. 132.
2. " 'The Reptile's Lot': Theme and Image in Coleridge's Later Poetry," p. 350.

or simply as a dream unrealized. Angela Dorenkamp has said of Coleridge's later years, "In retrospect, these years of primarily religious speculation illumine his entire life as a journey toward the Absolute."[3] While some of the later poems we shall consider here are primarily strategies for dealing with the loss of love, others are, sometimes in subtle ways, part of a movement toward the Absolute, which is the final goal of Coleridge's search for love.

*   *   *

A careful reading of one such poem, "Constancy to an Ideal Object," will reveal something of the complexity of Coleridge's view of love in these later years.[4] Because it is commonly grouped with Coleridge's "late poems"—which for many years received little critical attention—this poem has only in recent years begun to be seriously studied, as the late poems have come more and more into their own. I propose to approach the poem through the interpretations of three critics whose readings are clearly interrelated; I would like to suggest, in fact, that together they make up a history of the modern interpretation of this poem. After tracing the development of these three views, I shall venture to push the history onward a bit with some reflections of my own.

Most critics who have written of "Constancy to an Ideal Object" agree that it expresses Coleridge's deep sadness over his unfulfilled love of Sara Hutchinson. Beyond that, however, the divergences are considerable. James Boulger sees the poem as a product of what he calls Coleridge's "semidualism" in his later work. "The thinking Christian," Boulger wrote, "could no longer pursue his God through the analogies of Nature. Henceforth Coleridge's poetry was to be written in two moods, one looking backward mournfully upon the days when Nature had been his friend through the interpenetration of subject and object, the other looking forward, in hope but not enthusiasm, to the time when the soul would be able to free itself from matter for union with a highly intellectualized version of Divinity."[5] "Constancy to an Ideal Object" was written, Boulger believes, in the first of these moods, for here "the breakdown of interplay between spirit and Nature is complete" (p. 208). From the very opening of the poem, human thought is detached from the world; it is indeed "the only

---

3. "Hope at Highgate: The Late Poetry of S. T. Coleridge," p. 59.

4. Although the poem first appeared in Coleridge's three-volume *Poetical Works* of 1828, it remains a mystery how long before that it was written. For a long time (following Ernest Hartley Coleridge) it was conjecturally dated 1826, until the discovery that Coleridge refers to the poem in a letter of 1825 to Joseph Henry Green, asking Green to "procure me a Copy of those Lines which a long time ago I sent to Mrs. Green by you, on constancy to the *Idea* of a beloved Object—ending, I remember, with a Simile of a Woodman following his own projected Shadow" (*CL* 5:467 [11 June 1825]). James Dykes Campbell dated it as early as 1804, conjecturing—mainly, it seems, on the basis of the homesick-sounding line "To have a home, an English home, and thee!" (l. 18)—that it was probably written during Coleridge's year in Malta (quoted by Ernest Hartley Coleridge, *PW,* 1:455, note 1). More likely, I believe, is that it was written sometime after 1810, in the aftermath of Coleridge's final enforced separation from Sara Hutchinson following the rupture between Coleridge and Wordsworth.

5. *Coleridge as Religious Thinker,* pp. 207–8. In the discussion that follows, this work will be cited parenthetically in the text.

constant in a world of change" (l. 3). The poet does glance for a moment at the possible reunion of "thought with its object, man with Nature, Coleridge with Sara Hutchinson" (p. 209), but it remains a backward glance, expressed in terms of the nature imagery of such early poems as "Frost at Midnight" and "This Lime-Tree Bower My Prison"—expressing a unity no longer attainable:

> Vain repetition! Home and Thou are one.
> The peacefull'st cot, the moon shall shine upon,
> Lulled by the thrush and wakened by the lark . . .
>
> (ll. 19–21)

The poet quickly modulates back to the present, with the present divorce between man and nature represented by the same imagery used for the "spiritually isolated Mariner" (p. 209):

> Without thee were but a becalmèd bark,
> Whose Helmsman on an ocean waste and wide
> Sits mute and pale his mouldering helm beside.
>
> (ll. 22–24)

Boulger does allow for ambiguity at the end of the poem, but it is only the ambiguity of an unpalatable choice: "Either man is a spiritual creature involved in an ontological complex with his Creator, essentially apart from Nature, or else his highest nature is only the self-generated illusion of the rustic" (p. 210):

> An image with a glory round its head;
> The enamoured rustic worships its fair hues,
> Nor knows he makes the shadow, he pursues!
>
> (ll. 30–32)

There is no love, no hope, no joy. "The either/or cannot be bridged by the exuberance of poetic imagination" (p. 210).

Stephen Prickett offers a more subtly ambiguous analysis of the poem, which is probably truer to its complexity.[6] He begins with the closing metaphor of the poem, the so-called Brocken-spectre, the phenomenon of the mountain-traveler's shadow projected on the mist before him and appearing as an awesome figure with an aureole of light around its head:

> And art thou nothing? Such thou art, as when
> The woodman winding westward up the glen
> At wintry dawn, where o'er the sheep-track's maze
> The viewless snow-mist weaves a glist'ning haze,
> Sees full before him, gliding without tread,

6. *Coleridge and Wordsworth: The Poetry of Growth,* pp. 22–29. In the discussion that follows, this work will be cited parenthetically in the text.

An image with a glory round its head;
The enamoured rustic worships its fair hues,
Nor knows he makes the shadow, he pursues!
                    (ll. 25–32)

Here, as elsewhere in Coleridge's references to the experience of the Brocken-spectre, it is, Prickett suggests, "an image of a certain kind of ambiguity" (p. 23). Coleridge sees it also—and in particular—as an image of the creative experience. It is both himself and other than himself. As Prickett puts it, "One minute he is striving after an apparently objective ideal; in the next, it has become his own shadow on the mist" (p. 23). It is precisely this "ironic complexity" that made the image so appealing to Coleridge. As Coleridge wrote in a passage from *Aids to Reflection,* "The beholder either recognizes it as a projected form of his own being, that moves before him with a glory round its head, or recoils from it as from a spectre."[7]

For Prickett, "this symbol of the Brocken-spectre is central to Coleridge's thought about his own creativity" (p. 26). In the experience of the poet, as in the experience of the rustic woodman, "Coleridge's 'ideal object' is . . . both 'objective' and, at the same time, uniquely personal," for Coleridge has "chosen as his symbol a kind of experience where perception is in a peculiarly literal sense an act of creation" (p. 26). Therefore, this pursuit of an "ideal object" is not an abstraction, but a human experience, with a validity all its own: "The rustic is not the passive spectator; he pursues, and *by his own act of pursuit* gives life to his ideal" (p. 29).

Edward Kessler also focuses on the vision of the Brocken-spectre as the foundation of the poem.[8] This phenomenon is seen, here as elsewhere in Coleridge, as "a demonstration of the mind's power to transfigure actuality" (p. 128). Kessler sees "Constancy to an Ideal Object" as part of the aftermath of a "dissociation of sensibility" that had set in for Coleridge, the experience he had confronted in "Dejection: An Ode," the dissociation of thought from the external world. His search from then on was a quest for Being, for "the original unity of thought and thing." It was a search to find again "the 'one Life' that he had shattered by 'abstruse research'" (p. 124). The means he found to do this was (in Coleridge's own words) "to emancipate the mind from the despotism of the eye."[9] It was, in effect, to use what we call "abstraction" to discover the deeper sense of Being. As Kessler puts it, "Abstraction can be a repository for experience, a 'form for feeling,' and a means of discovering a new self" (p. 125).[10] Thus there opens up the possibility of using an experience of loss of physical presence—in this case the loss of Sara—as a means of achieving a deeper kind of presence, so that loss becomes gain.

7. *Aids,* p. 249, note.

8. *Coleridge's Metaphors of Being,* pp. 127–37. In the discussion that follows, this work will be cited parenthetically in the text.

9. Alice D. Snyder, *Coleridge on Logic and Learning,* pp. 126–27; quoted by Kessler, *Coleridge's Metaphors of Being,* p. 125.

10. This view of the uses of abstraction contrasts tellingly with Patricia M. Adair's indictment of most of Coleridge's later poetry for its "dismaying abstraction"; see *The Waking Dream: A Study of Coleridge's Poetry,* pp. 222–26. The phrase quoted is on p. 225.

Kessler's strategy is, in effect, to project back on the earlier part of the poem (the poet's attempt to articulate his vision of the beloved "ideal object") the *process* he sees operating in the vision of the Brocken-spectre, by which literal reality is transformed into an ideal—while keeping something of its literal actuality. For what the poet has come to realize is that "his ideal object is the *thought* of Sara rather than her physical presence, it is *love* and not love's embodiment" (p. 131). The woodman is thus an analogue of the poet in his transforming of actuality into ideality: "In contrast to the stagnant, passive Being represented by the 'mute' and 'pale' Helmsman who cannot progress toward any meaningful goal, the Woodman at the end of the poem is filled with Hope, and the final lines of the poem register activity, an energy that makes thought vital" (p. 135). In short, then, "through the 'life-enkindling' power of the poet's imagination, his abstractions are reclaimed from pure thought and returned to the life that fostered them" (p. 136).

Thus, I would add, the crucial question that begins the Woodman section—"And art thou nothing?"—is not, as has commonly been assumed, a rhetorical question. Rather, it implies that the poet's experience of his "ideal object" is real: as real as the Woodman's encounter with the Brocken-spectre, but a reality made up of both subjective and objective experience. Therefore, what the poem affirms (returning to Kessler), is that art "can bring thoughts and things—experience itself—into a temporary form, a shape for Being. In a work of art, the imaginative viewer can discover both himself and his transfigured self" (p. 136). As Coleridge himself said of the plays of Shakespeare: "In the plays of Shakespeare every man sees himself, without knowing that he does so: as in some of the phenomena of nature, in the mist of the mountain, the traveler beholds his own figure, but the glory round the head distinguishes it from a mere vulgar copy."[11] "The ideal object," Kessler concludes, "is finally not an object, but a subject that has been realized" (p. 137).

I suggested at the outset that these three interpretations—by Boulger, Prickett, and Kessler—are interrelated. It is clear that each of the later critics was aware of and reacting to the earlier. There is a sense, as in much of the best criticism, of movement in a direction, with a deeper understanding at the end of the process.

Boulger's reading is essentially negative, seeing the poem in the context of later poems that are read as reflective of a Coleridge who had lost hope, who was hopelessly immersed in a "semidualism" that essentially divorced thought from the object of thought. In such a reading, the "ideal object" could remain only a lifeless abstraction, and "constancy" to such an object was fruitless. Prickett was able to move beyond this merely negative reading to a more complex sense of the ambiguity of the poem, so that he was able to affirm the *existential* character of the experience—both the experience of the poet's transformation of Sara into an ideal Sara and its metaphoric counterpart, the experience of the Brocken-spectre. This complex experience, in other words, has *value* precisely as a human and aesthetic experience. Kessler, for his part, building on the insights of Prickett, was able to go even further, to see the experience as a *process,* so that the ending of the poem is open to the future—and is therefore a sign of hope.

What Boulger, Prickett, and Kessler have all done—quite brilliantly—is to focus

---

11. *SC,* 2:125; quoted by Kessler, *Coleridge's Metaphors of Being,* p. 136.

on the epistemological significance of the poem. There is, however, another level of meaning that has been relatively neglected: the personal level—the lament for Coleridge's very real, lost Sara. This level remains the first level of meaning: the personal lament for the loss of a beloved woman. As biblical scholars insist in their own discipline, all the meanings of a text must be grounded in the literal meaning.

I suggest, then, that the poem exists on two conflicting levels, which (paradoxically) co-exist in fruitful tension. The first level, the personal lament of the poet (not as poet but as lover) for his lost love—a very real loss evoking sadness, frustration, and anguish—accounts for the ordinary reader's unquestionable sense of the poem as a lament and of its ending, the rustic woodman's self-deception, as a kind of mocking irony. On a more sophisticated (though not necessarily deeper) level, there is the poem written by the poet not as lover but as poet: an entranced, even triumphant, awareness of the process of his own thought. Unlike the rustic woodman, the poet is *aware* of the process and (paradoxically, given the sad occasion for the poem) delights in it.

The question is one of vision. The lover of the poem, like the woodman, has only single vision. The woodman sees only his shadow with a glory round its head, and worships it as something divine. The lover sees only his own loss, and mourns for it. The poet, however, unlike both of them, has double vision. Unlike the woodman, the poet knows that what he sees is only a shadow and that there is a light that casts the shadow; he knows that the sun is a cause of both the shadow and the glorious aureole. He knows that the phenomenon is both from himself and from the sun; of his own making and not of his own making. Unlike the lover, the poet knows not only the loss of love but also the triumph of artistic transformation by which the actual becomes ideal. Just as the poet is aware of both shadow and sun, so is he aware of both loss and achievement, pain and aesthetic joy.

The poem can surely be read, then—as Prickett and Kessler do—as a drama of the transformation of pain into art. Let me continue the earlier quotation from Coleridge on Shakespeare, which suggests something of this transformation: "So in Shakespeare: every form is true, everything has reality for its foundation; we can all recognize the truth, but we see it decorated with such hues of beauty, and magnified to such proportions of grandeur, that, while we know the figure, we know also how much it has been refined and exalted by the poet."[12] Surely in "Constancy to an Ideal Object" the truth is pain, the very real pain of loss; but it is pain transfigured by art—in Coleridge's words, "refined and exalted" by the poet. Yet the pain one senses at the end of the poem is still very much a personal lament for a very real beloved. What Prickett and Kessler see as a "transformation" of pain into art is rather, I suggest, a "fusing" of the two into a symbol of both, in which personal pain and artistic triumph interpenetrate one another—the personal and the philosophical values coming together, consubstantial one with the other. Surely pain is transmuted by the artistic process into wonder at the "glory"—yet the pain remains, idealized but real, glorified but aching.

At the same time, it must not be forgotten that the poet has found not only "love's embodiment" but also ideal love itself, and in doing so he has discovered that the source of ideal love is beyond himself: its representation in "glory" is not only from himself but also from the sun—the *natura naturans,* the burning fountain. In this moment he and the source of all light have found each other; he has touched the Absolute—or rather, perhaps, the Absolute has touched him—even though it happens as much in darkness as in light, even though the sunlight is filtered through the mountain mist.

*   *   *

But this momentary touch of the Absolute, the "ideal love," was not a steady presence for Coleridge during these years, and other poems of the period reveal an ambivalence that is both deep and far-ranging. "Recollections of Love" (1807), for example, finds human love bound up with the poet's affection for nature:

> How warm this woodland wild Recess!
>   Love surely hath been breathing here;
>   And this sweet bed of heath, my dear!
> Swells up, then sinks with faint caress,
>   As if to have you yet more near.
>   (ll. 1–5)

It was here, "eight springs" ago (l. 6), that the poet first had intimations of the beloved woman who was to enter his life; in this scene he had found a "sense of promise everywhere" (l. 14). She was first known as an ideal to be striven for, "a thought" or "dream" still to be realized, and then in this place first made real. Little wonder, then, that this is a beloved place, the Greta a beloved stream.

> You stood before me like a thought,
>   A dream remembered in a dream.
>   But when those meek eyes first did seem
> To tell me, Love within you wrought—
>   O Greta, dear domestic stream!
>   (ll. 21–25)

Since then the voice of this landscape—the sound of this stream—has brought joy and peace. Love seems, indeed, as sustaining and steady as nature itself:

> Has not, since then, Love's prompture deep,
>   Has not Love's whisper evermore
>   Been ceaseless, as thy gentle roar?
> Sole voice, when other voices sleep,
>   Dear under-song in clamor's hour.
>   (ll. 26–30)

But for all the sense of peace, there are subtly disquieting notes. Although "Love's prompture" is deep, it is difficult to forget that the actual beloved woman is present only "like a thought," like "a dream remembered in a dream." Although the poet professes to hear "Love's whisper evermore," it is in fact the "gentle roar" of the stream he hears. The landscape is real; the woman, alas, is not. Not least of all, although the stream is gentle, it is heard not in a moment of peace but in "clamor's hour."

More than a decade later, in the sonnet "To Nature" (?1820), Coleridge still found "lessons of love" in nature:

> It may indeed be phantasy, when I
> Essay to draw from all created things
> Deep, heartfelt, inward joy that closely clings;
> And trace in leaves and flowers that round me lie
> Lessons of love and earnest piety.
> So let it be; and if the wide world rings
> In mock of this belief, it brings
> Nor fear, nor grief, nor vain perplexity.
> So will I build my altar in the fields,
> And the blue sky my fretted dome shall be,
> And the sweet fragrance that the wild flower yields
> Shall be the incense I will yield to Thee,
> Thee only God! and thou shalt not despise
> Even me, the priest of this poor sacrifice.

The sonnet begins with a typically Coleridgean moment of self-doubt: he "essays" to find joy in nature, and even that attempt may be only a "phantasy." This is far from the self-confidence of Wordsworth, who would have drawn his lessons from nature unhesitatingly and without apology; but this is Coleridge, whose joy is invariably harder won. The doubts are soon set aside, however, if not wholly overcome: "so let it be," which in the context of what is to follow one might almost interpret as "Amen!" For the sestet does become a kind of act of faith, appropriately taking the form of a scene of worship in the open air: the altar, the dome of sky, the wildflower incense, and the priest-poet offering his sacrifice. Also appropriately, the movement is toward an encounter between the poet-priest and his God—perhaps intimating the nature of the more religious consolation toward which Coleridge himself was moving. But this poet is a humbler priest than Wordsworth, who in his guise of "Nature's priest" would hardly have thought of either his poetry or his praise as "this poor sacrifice." The word *yield,* quietly repeated, suggests in fact the increasingly humble "yielding" of Coleridge to a power greater than himself.

* * *

However, even this modest solace in nature was not lasting, and Angela Dorenkamp is surely right when she says of Coleridge's late poems generally that "the disengagement of Nature and spirit eliminated for Coleridge a major source of hope."[13]

13. Dorenkamp, "Hope at Highgate," p. 60.

However, the longing for hope remained a frequent theme, and other late poems reveal both a bond and a struggle between hope and love. "The Visionary Hope" (?1810), for example, suggests how tenuous hope of love can be for one who has suffered the loss of love. Though hope was "his inward bliss and boast, / Which waned and died, yet ever near him stood," it had little with which to console him, "for Love's Despair is but Hope's pining Ghost!" (ll. 17–20). But hope remained alive in spite of all his suffering, for he concludes:

> yet this one Hope should give
> Such strength that he would bless his pains and live.
> (ll. 27–28)

"Youth and Age" (1823–1832) might seem at first to be fairly simple in its dramatic structure—a movement from the joys of youth to the burdens of old age—turning about the early brief line "When I was young," which is echoed in "Ere I was old" and at last reaches definitive closure in "When we are old." But a more careful reading reveals a complex dialectic at work in the poem, a struggle between the spirit of youth and the burdened spirit of age. At first,

> Life went a-maying
> With Nature, Hope, and Poesy,
> When I was young!
> (ll. 3–5)

At once, however, the voice of age interjects:

> When I was young?—Ah, woful When!
> Ah! for the change 'twixt Now and Then!
> This breathing house not built with hands,
> This body that does me grievous wrong.
> (ll. 6–9)

But immediately the evocation of the body begins to recall its past delights:

> O'er aery cliffs and glittering sands,
> How lightly then it flashed along.
> (ll. 10–11)

And the last lines of this stanza are an almost triumphant celebration of strength and joy:

> Nought cared this body for wind or weather
> When Youth and I lived in't together,
> (ll. 16–17)

It is out of this joy that we hear the most charming and delicate lines of the poem:

Flowers are lovely; Love is flower-like;
Friendship is a sheltering tree;
O! the joys, that came down shower-like,
Of Friendship, Love, and Liberty,
                    Ere I was old!
                        (ll. 18–22)

Once again, this last line calls the poet back to present reality: "Ere I was old? Ah woful
Ere, / Which tells me, Youth's no longer here!" (ll. 23–24).

This time the poet will attempt to escape the present not by the use of memory but
by self-deception: old age is only a "strange disguise" that hides his real self, which still
has "Spring-tide blossoms" on his lips and "sunshine" in his eyes (ll. 31–36).

Life is but thought: so think I will
That Youth and I are house-mates still.
                    (ll. 37–38)

But pretense cannot conceal the truth: old age is not a mask; it is the present reality.
He may be the same person, but old age is not youth:

Dew-drops are the gems of morning,
But the tears of mournful eve!
                    (ll. 39–40)

Finally, pretense is not only false but is also perceived as sadly false by all who see it.
Like the guest who has outworn his welcome, old age "tells the jest without the smile"
(l. 49). One may wear the mask of youth, but the spirit of youth has gone. Now,
significantly, it is all of us who share the poet's experience: it is no longer "I" but
"we"—"when *we* are old."

In "Love, Hope, and Patience in Education" (1829), the poet at first believes that
love and hope can sustain each other:

O part them never! If Hope prostrate lie,
        Love too will sink and die.
But Love is subtle, and doth proof derive
From her own life that Hope is yet alive;
And bending o'er, with soul-transfusing eyes,
And the soft murmurs of the mother dove,
Woos back the fleeting spirit, and half supplies;—
Thus Love repays to Hope what Hope first gave to Love.
                    (ll. 13–20)

Clearly, although hope and love are mutually dependent, love is here the power on
which the poet most relies; love is indeed the "proof" that there is hope. Love is, too, a
nurturing power, and it is significant that it is imaged in its maternal aspect ("the
mother dove"), given the primal role Coleridge gives to maternal love in the development of the affective life.

But even love's power is not without limit, and love and hope may one day have to yield to patience:

> Yet haply there will come a weary day,
>> When overtask'd at length
> Both Love and Hope beneath the load give way.
> Then with a statue's smile, a statue's strength,
> Stands the mute sister, Patience, nothing loth,
> And both supporting does the work of both.
>> (ll. 21–26)

The outcome is ambiguous at best, for all its tone of quiet acceptance. The reigning power is no longer Love, whose eyes are "soul-transfusing" and who can at least murmur comfortingly in a mother's role, but "the mute sister, Patience." The "light of happy faces" (l. 2) that opened the poem has now been replaced by "a statue's smile," and what was living power is now the strength of a statue. For the moment at least, the poet's voice has been stilled.

* * *

The touching sonnet "Duty Surviving Self-Love" (1826), on the other hand, suggests a return of the poet's ability to affirm the ideal of love. The poem was preceded in the original draft (though not in its published form) by a charming introductory fiction, in which Alia asks the old philosopher Constantius if he is happier because of his philosophy. "And the smile of Constantius was as the light from a purple cluster of the vine, gleaming through snowflakes, as he replied, The Boons of Philosophy are of higher worth, than what you, O Alia, mean by Happiness."[14] Continuing to reflect on Alia's question after she leaves, Constantius gives voice to a soliloquy in the form of this sonnet:

> Unchanged within, to see all changed without,
> Is a blank lot and hard to bear, no doubt.
> Yet why at others' wanings should'st thou fret?
> Then only might'st thou feel a just regret,
> Hadst thou withheld thy love or hid thy light
> In selfish forethought of neglect and slight.
> O wiselier then, from feeble yearnings freed,
> While, and on whom, thou may'st—shine on! nor heed
> Whether the object by reflected light
> Return thy radiance or absorb it quite:
> And though thou notest from thy safe recess
> Old Friends burn dim, like lamps in noisome air,
> Love them for what they are; nor love them less,
> Because to thee they are not what they were.

14. *PW,* 1:459.

It is possible, I suppose, to read this sonnet as the poet's dedication to the abstractions of philosophy in place of lost love. The nobility of tone, however—of both the poem and the introduction—suggests something much deeper, and indeed "of higher worth": a turning away from reliance on others or on outward objects for meaning to an acceptance of one's own chosen ideal. It is a long step toward maturity in love, a gracious movement toward selflessness and generosity of spirit. As he had learned at last to accept unconditional love in his life, so here (as at the end of "Dejection") the poet is able to affirm the nobility of *giving* such love: "Love them for what they are; nor love them less, / Because to thee they are not what they were." Love does not cease to be love simply because it is not requited. And the very thought of this ideal can be sustaining: "While, and on whom, thou may'st—shine on!" This is not, to be sure, a grasp on the Absolute, but as an affirmation of an ideal love it is surely a movement in its direction.

"The Improvisatore," written a year later, does not intimate anything as grand as Coleridge's drive toward the Absolute, but it does sketch out—in a sometimes playful dramatic form—his retrospective view of true love, especially married love, and his acceptance of his present limitations.[15]

Katherine, one of the characters in the prose dialogue, suggests that true love would be "A precious boon, that would go far to reconcile one to old age—this love—*if* true! But is there any such true love?" (p. 463). The elderly sage, the "Friend," concludes that "Love, truly such, is itself not the most common thing in the world: and mutual love still less so" (p. 464). Between husband and wife especially can come faults that too often prove to be "the dead fly in the compost of spices" (p. 465).[16] Turning then to poetry, the Friend improvises a verse that portrays his own earlier hopes for love and his ultimate disappointment:

> Doubts toss'd him to and fro:
> Hope keeping Love, Love Hope alive,
> Like babes bewildered in a snow,
> That cling and huddle from the cold
> In hollow tree or ruin'd fold.
>   (ll. 30–34)

At last he comes to realize, in his old age, that such love is no longer his: "Whate'er it *was,* it *is* no longer so" (l. 62). Yet his response is not despair but, perhaps curiously, contentment:

> Though heart be lonesome, Hope laid low,
> Yet, Lady! deem him not unblest:
> The certainty that struck Hope dead,
> Hath left Contentment in her stead:
>   And that is next to Best!
>   (ll. 63–67)

---

15. *PW,* 1:462–68. This prose dialogue will hereafter be cited in the text by its page number in *PW.*
16. See Ecclesiastes 10:1.

The Improvisatore does not give the source of this contentment, but he does offer an image that suggests something of its emotional content: although the "sovran Rose" of "life's gay summer" has passed (l. 55), there still remains "Late autumn's Amaranth, that more fragrant blows / When Passion's flowers all fall or fade" (ll. 56–57). Here is a kind of calm acceptance, reminiscent of Wordsworth's "philosophic mind" that finds "strength in what remains behind," "in the faith that looks through death"—or in Keats's reassurance to Autumn, "thou hast thy music too." It is as if now that he knows the struggle is over ("Passion's flowers" have fallen or faded), the poet can be at peace. Such contentment cannot offer the fulfillment true married or romantic love can bring, but it is "next to Best!" He may no longer be a "lover," but it is significant that the poet can still cast himself in the role of "Friend."

The year before he died, Coleridge wrote one of the darkest of his poems on love, "Love's Apparition and Evanishment" (1833). The poet sees himself "like a lone Arab, old and blind, / Some caravan had left behind" (ll. 1–2). Unable to see and hearing no human voice, he turns inward and there finds "Hope, / Love's elder sister," dressed as a bridesmaid, but "lifeless," "all pale and cold" (ll. 17–21).

> And then came Love, a sylph in bridal trim,
>   And stood beside my seat;
> She bent, and kiss'd her sister's lips,
>   As she was wont to do;—
> Alas! 'twas but a chilling breath
> Woke just enough of life in death
>   To make Hope die anew.
>   (ll. 22–28)

Once again we see how love and hope are interdependent. Without hope, love can offer only "a chilling breath" with her kiss; without the warmth of fulfilled love, hope can come to life only for a fleeting moment.[17]

* * *

It is clear, as we have seen earlier in this study, that Coleridge did not lack for love during this period of his life, especially during the long years at Highgate. They were in fact years richly blessed with friendship. However, I suggest that Coleridge's increasingly strong sense of coming to the end of his life made him feel deeply at times

17. Four lines that were added after Coleridge's death simply underscore the darkness of the vision:

> In vain we supplicate the Powers above;
> There is no resurrection for the Love
> That, nursed in tenderest care, yet fades away
> In the chill'd heart by gradual self-decay.

In the earliest extant version of the poem, these lines are found at the beginning of the poem (*PW,* 2:1087–88), but they do not appear in the version published by Coleridge in 1834. They were added as "L'Envoy" in 1852; see *PW,* 1:488, note 3.

his lack of a single emotional focus, such as a wife or a romantic attachment would have given him. This sense of ending was not from any fear of death, but rather from a realization that he was coming to the end with so much—both in his life and in his work—yet undone. An emotional center for his life would perhaps have given him the kind of sense of "completeness" he was never able to achieve. However, effectively countering this lack of a human emotional focus was his effort to live more and more "in God"—not rejecting those he loved by any means, but seeing them more and more in terms of his and their finitude and finality. The following notebook entry of 1830 (which we have already seen in another context) beautifully reveals this attitude:

> The Crown and Base, the Pinnacle and Foundation of a regenerate and truly Christian State of Mind, as long as our Souls are within the fleshly veil, is to love God in all that we love, to love that only therefore in which we can at the same time love God—and thus gradually, in the growth toward our final perfection, more and more to love all things in God.[18]

Just days before his death, Coleridge wrote a letter, the last of his letters still extant (apart from a touching note a few hours before he died, in which he commended a faithful servant, Harriet Macklin, to the generosity of his heirs), addressed to his year-old godson, Adam Steinmetz Kinnaird. Writing, as he says, "on the brink of the grave," he "solemnly bears witness" that God "is faithful to perform what He has promised, & has preserved under all my pains & infirmities, the inward peace that passeth all understanding." He concludes: "O my dear Godchild! eminently blessed are they who begin *early* to seek, fear, & love their God, trusting wholly in the righteousness & mediation of their Lord, Redeemer, Saviour, & everlasting High Priest, Jesus Christ."[19]

Coleridge's touching emphasis on "early" suggests his belief that he himself had begun late to love God. One might think of Augustine's cry of the heart: "Late have I loved thee, O Beauty ancient and ever new." What happened, I suggest, both in Coleridge's life and in his poetry, was that in his later years the focus of his quest became more and more fixed on God. His loving friends did not leave him, nor did he forget them; but more and more his eyes were fixed on the Eternal Love that drew him. As he had written years before, "There is a capaciousness in every *living* Heart, which retains an aching Vacuum . . . God only can *fill* it."[20] But it was, as always, a humble Coleridge who faced his Maker at the end. His very epitaph, composed the year before he died, reflects that humility—along with a touch of his eternal Esteeseean playfulness.

Stop, Christian passer-by!—Stop, child of God,
And read with gentle breast. Beneath this sod
A poet lies, or that which once seem'd he.
O, lift one thought in prayer for S.T.C.;
That he who many a year with toil of breath
Found death in life, may here find life in death!
Mercy for praise—to be forgiven for fame
He ask'd, and hoped, through Christ. Do thou the same!

18. Notebook 47, f. 3 (1 October 1830).
19. *CL,* 6:990 (13 July 1834).
20. *CL,* 4:607 (25 October 1815).

At the end, he asks mercy and forgiveness. Not love? But surely yes. Only a year before he had written: "The Love of an almighty I AM to a fallen & suffering Spirit becomes Mercy. To Spirits Conformed to the Holy Will the I AM is the God of *Love*— to a fallen Spirit the God of *Mercy*. Love and Mercy are the same attribute differenced only by the difference in the Objects."[21] So this loving man, strong in his weakness, died trusting in the power of a Love greater than his own. It was, finally, in God that Coleridge found the fulfillment of his lifelong yearning for love. Gillman and Green were with him when he died—representing, I like to think, all those who loved him and whom he so dearly loved—but it was at last into God's hands that he yielded his great spirit.

---

21. Notebook F, f. 85v (6 March 1832).

WORKS CITED

Abrams, M. H. "The Correspondent Breeze: A Romantic Metaphor." In *English Romantic Poets: Modern Essays in Criticism,* edited by M. H. Abrams, pp. 37–54. 2d ed. New York: Oxford University Press, 1975.

———. *Natural Supernaturalism: Tradition and Revolution in Romantic Literature.* New York: W. W. Norton, 1971.

———. "Structure and Style in the Greater Romantic Lyric." In *Romanticism and Consciousness: Essays in Criticism,* edited by Harold Bloom, pp. 201–29. New York: W. W. Norton, 1970.

Adair, Patricia M. *The Waking Dream: A Study of Coleridge's Poetry.* New York: Barnes and Noble, 1967.

Alexander, Meena. *The Poetic Self: Towards a Phenomenology of Romanticism.* New Delhi: Arnold-Heinemann, 1979.

Barth, J. Robert, S.J. *Coleridge and Christian Doctrine.* Cambridge: Harvard University Press, 1969.

———. *The Symbolic Imagination: Coleridge and the Romantic Tradition.* Princeton: Princeton University Press, 1977.

———. "Theological Implications of Coleridge's Theory of Imagination." *Studies in the Literary Imagination* 19 (1986): 23–33.

Bate, Walter Jackson. *Coleridge.* New York: Macmillan, 1968.

Beer, John. *Coleridge the Visionary.* New York: Collier Books, 1962.

———. *Coleridge's Poetic Intelligence.* London: Macmillan, 1977.

———. *Wordsworth and the Human Heart.* New York: Columbia University Press, 1978.

Beres, David. "A Dream, A Vision, and a Poem: A Psycho-Analytic Study of the Origins of *The Rime of the Ancient Mariner.*" *International Journal of Psycho-Analysis* 32 (1951): 97–116.

Bernhardt-Kabisch, Ernest. *Robert Southey.* Boston: Twayne, 1977.

Blake, William. *The Complete Poetry and Prose of William Blake.* Edited by David V. Erdman. Berkeley: University of California Press, 1982.

Boulger, James D. *Coleridge as Religious Thinker.* New Haven: Yale University Press, 1961.

Bouslog, Charles. "Structure and Theme in Coleridge's 'Dejection: An Ode.'" *Modern Language Quarterly* 24 (1963): 42–52.

Broughton, Panthea Reid. "The Modifying Metaphor in 'Dejection: An Ode.'" *The Wordsworth Circle* 4 (1973): 241–49.

Byron, George Gordon, Lord. *The Complete Poetical Works.* Edited by Jerome J. McGann. 3 vols. Oxford: Clarendon Press, 1980.

———. *The Selected Poetry of Lord Byron.* Edited by Leslie A. Marchand. New York: Modern Library, 1954.

Chambers, E. K. *Samuel Taylor Coleridge: A Biographical Study.* Oxford: Clarendon Press, 1938.

Chayes, Irene H. "Rhetoric as Drama: An Approach to the Romantic Ode." *PMLA* 79 (1964): 67–79.

Coleridge, Samuel Taylor. *Aids to Reflection in the formation of a manly character on the several grounds of prudence, morality and religion, illustrated by select passages from our elder divines, especially from Archbishop Leighton.* Edited by Henry Nelson Coleridge. In *The Complete Works,* ed. Shedd, vol. 1.

———. *Biographia Literaria.* Edited by James Engell and W. Jackson Bate. In *The Collected Works,* ed. Coburn, vol. 7. 2 vols. Princeton: Princeton University Press, 1983.

———. *Biographia Literaria.* Edited by J. Shawcross. 2 vols. Oxford: Oxford University Press, 1907.

———. *Collected Letters of Samuel Taylor Coleridge.* Edited by Earl Leslie Griggs. 6 vols. Oxford: Clarendon Press, 1956–1971.

———. *The Collected Works of Samuel Taylor Coleridge.* Edited by Kathleen Coburn. Princeton: Princeton University Press, 1969– . (Bollingen Series LXXV.)

———. *The Complete Poetical Works of Samuel Taylor Coleridge.* Edited by Ernest Hartley Coleridge. 2 vols. Oxford: Clarendon Press, 1912.

———. *The Complete Works of Samuel Taylor Coleridge, with an Introductory Essay upon His Philosophical and Theological Opinions.* Edited by W. G. T. Shedd. 7 vols. New York: Harper and Brothers, 1856.

———. *The Friend: A Series of Essays To Aid in the Formation of Fixed Principles in Politics, Morals, and Religion, with Literary Amusements Interspersed.* Edited by Barbara E. Rooke. In *The Collected Works,* ed. Coburn, vol. 4. 2 vols. Princeton: Princeton University Press, 1969.

———. *Lay Sermons.* Edited by R. J. White. In *The Collected Works,* ed. Coburn, vol. 6. London: Routledge & Kegan Paul, 1972.

———. *Lectures 1795: On Politics and Religion.* Edited by Lewis Patton and Peter Mann. In *The Collected Works,* ed. Coburn, vol. 1. London: Routledge & Kegan Paul, 1971.

———. *The Literary Remains of Samuel Taylor Coleridge.* Edited by Henry Nelson Coleridge. In *The Complete Works,* ed. Shedd, vol. 5.

———. *Logic.* Edited by J. R. de J. Jackson. In *The Collected Works,* ed. Coburn, vol. 13. Princeton: Princeton University Press, 1981.

———. *Marginalia.* Edited by George Whalley. In *The Collected Works,* ed. Coburn, vol. 12. 2 vols to date. Princeton: Princeton University Press, 1980– .

———. *The Notebooks of Samuel Taylor Coleridge.* Edited by Kathleen Coburn. 3 vols to date. Bollingen Series L. New York: Pantheon, 1957– ; Princeton: Princeton University Press, 1973.

———. *Notes and Lectures upon Shakespeare and Some of the Old Poets and Dramatists, with Other Literary Remains.* Edited by Mrs. H. N. Coleridge. In *The Complete Works,* ed. Shedd, vol. 4.

———. *Philosophical Lectures.* Edited by Kathleen Coburn. New York: Philosophical Library, 1949.

———. *Poems.* Edited by John Beer. London: J. M. Dent, Everyman's Library, 1974.

———. *Shakespearean Criticism.* Edited by Thomas Middleton Raysor. 2 vols. London: J. M. Dent, Everyman's Library, 1960.

———. *Specimens of the Table Talk of the Late Samuel Taylor Coleridge.* Edited by Henry Nelson Coleridge. In *The Complete Works,* ed. Shedd, vol. 6.

Dekker, George. *Coleridge and the Literature of Sensibility.* New York: Barnes and Noble, 1978.

Dickstein, Morris. "Coleridge, Wordsworth, and the 'Conversation Poems.'" *Centennial Review* 16 (1972): 367–83.

Dorenkamp, Angela G. "Hope at Highgate: The Late Poetry of S. T. Coleridge." *Barat Review* 6 (1971): 59–67.

Eliot, T. S. *Four Quartets.* Rev. ed. London: Faber & Faber, 1979.

Enscoe, Gerald. *Eros and the Romantics: Sexual Love as a Theme in Coleridge, Shelley and Keats.* The Hague: Mouton, 1967.

Fields, Beverly. *Reality's Dark Dream: Dejection in Coleridge.* Kent, Ohio: Kent State University Press, 1967.

Fogle, Richard Harter. "The Dejection of Coleridge's Ode." *English Literary History* 17 (1950): 71–77.

———. *The Idea of Coleridge's Criticism.* Perspectives in Criticism, 9. Berkeley: University of California Press, 1962.

Gillman, James. *The Life of Samuel Taylor Coleridge.* London: William Pickering, 1838.

Griggs, Earl Leslie. *Coleridge Fille: A Biography of Sara Coleridge.* London: Oxford University Press, 1940.

Harding, Anthony John. *Coleridge and the Idea of Love: Aspects of Relationship in Coleridge's Thought and Writing.* London: Cambridge University Press, 1974.

———. "Mythopoeic Elements in 'Christabel.'" *Modern Language Quarterly* 44 (1983): 39–50.

Harper, George McLean. "Coleridge's Conversation Poems." In *English Romantic Poets: Modern Essays in Criticism,* edited by M. H. Abrams, pp. 188–201. 2d ed. New York: Oxford University Press, 1975.

Haven, Richard. *Patterns of Consciousness: An Essay on Coleridge.* Amherst: The University of Massachusetts Press, 1969.

House, Humphry. *Coleridge: The Clark Lectures, 1951–52.* London: Rupert Hart-Davis, 1953.

Hunting, Constance. "Another Look at the 'Conclusion to Part II' of Christabel." *English Language Notes* 12 (1975): 171–76.

Keats, John. *The Letters of John Keats.* Edited by Hyder E. Rollins. Cambridge: Harvard University Press, 1958.

———. *The Poems of John Keats.* Edited by Jack Stillinger. Cambridge: Belknap Press of Harvard University Press, 1978.

Kelly, Patrick. "Day and Night: Mystery and Error in Coleridge's 'The Rime of the Ancient Mariner.'" *English Studies in Canada* 11 (1985): 295–310.

Kessler, Edward. *Coleridge's Metaphors of Being.* Princeton: Princeton University Press, 1979.

Lamb, Charles and Mary. *The Letters of Charles and Mary Lamb.* Edited by E. V. Lucas. 3 vols. London: J. M. Dent & Methuen & Co., 1935.

Lefebure, Molly. *The Bondage of Love: A Life of Mrs. Samuel Taylor Coleridge.* London: Victor Gollancz, 1986.

———. "'Toujours Gai': Mrs. Samuel Taylor Coleridge, 'A Most Extraordinary Character', Reviewed in the Light of Her Letters." *The Charles Lamb Bulletin,* n.s. 30 (April 1980): 105–20.

Magnuson, Paul. *Coleridge's Nightmare Poetry.* Charlottesville: University Press of Virginia, 1974.

Mahoney, John L. "'The Reptile's Lot': Theme and Image in Coleridge's Later Poetry." *The Wordsworth Circle* 8 (1977): 349–60.

McFarland, Thomas. *Romanticism and the Forms of Ruin: Wordsworth, Coleridge, and Modalities of Fragmentation.* Princeton: Princeton University Press, 1981.

Muirhead, John H. *Coleridge as Philosopher.* London: George Allen & Unwin, 1930.

Nethercot, Arthur H. *The Road to Tryermaine.* New York: Russell and Russell, 1962.

Parker, Reeve. *Coleridge's Meditative Art.* Ithaca: Cornell University Press, 1975.

Perkins, David, ed. *English Romantic Writers.* New York: Harcourt, Brace and World, 1967.

Prickett, Stephen. *Coleridge and Wordsworth: The Poetry of Growth.* Cambridge: Cambridge University Press, 1970.

Schulz, Max F. "Coleridge." In *The English Romantic Poets: A Review of Research and Criticism,* edited by Frank Jordan, pp. 341–463. 3d. ed. New York: Modern Language Association of America, 1972.

———. *The Poetic Voices of Coleridge.* Detroit: Wayne State University Press, 1964.

Shelley, Percy Bysshe. *Shelley's Poetry and Prose.* Edited by Donald H. Reiman and Sharon B. Powers. New York: W. W. Norton, 1977.

———. *Shelley's Prose.* Edited by David Lee Clark. Albuquerque: University of New Mexico Press, 1954.

Siegel, Robert. "The Serpent and the Dove: The Problem of Evil in Coleridge's Poetry." Ph.D. diss., Harvard University, 1968.

Simmons, Jack. *Southey.* London: Collins, 1945.

Smith, Fred Manning. "The Relation of Coleridge's *Ode on Dejection* to Wordsworth's *Ode on Intimations of Immortality*." *PMLA* 50 (1935): 224–34.

Snyder, Alice D. *Coleridge on Logic and Learning*. New Haven: Yale University Press, 1929.

Southey, Robert. *New Letters of Robert Southey*. Edited by Kenneth Curry. 2 vols. New York: Columbia University Press, 1965.

Spatz, Jonas. "Sexual Initiation in Coleridge's 'Christabel.'" *PMLA* 90 (1975): 107–16.

Suther, Marshall. *The Dark Night of Samuel Taylor Coleridge*. New York: Columbia University Press, 1960.

Watson, George. *Coleridge the Poet*. London: Routledge and Kegan Paul, 1966.

Whalley, George. *Coleridge and Sara Hutchinson*. Toronto: University of Toronto Press, 1955.

———. "The Mariner and the Albatross." In *Coleridge: A Collection of Critical Essays*, edited by Kathleen Coburn, pp. 32–50. Englewood Cliffs: Prentice-Hall, 1967.

Wordsworth, Christopher. *Memoirs of William Wordsworth, Poet-Laureate, D.C.L.* 2 vols. London: Edward Moxon, 1851.

Wordsworth, William. *The Poetical Works of William Wordsworth*. Edited by Ernest de Selincourt and Helen Darbishire. 5 vols. Oxford: Clarendon Press, 1940–1949.

———. *The Prelude*. Edited by Jonathan Wordsworth, M. H. Abrams, and Stephen Gill. New York: W. W. Norton, 1979.

Wordsworth, William and Dorothy. *The Letters of William and Dorothy Wordsworth*. 2d ed. 6 vols to date. Oxford: Clarendon Press, 1967–.

Index